Oxford Shakespeare Topics

GENERAL EDITORS: PETER HOLLAND AND STANLEY WELLS

Shakespeare, Race, and Colonialism

ANIA LOOMBA

OXFORD

UNIVERSITY PRESS

OXFORD

UNIVERSITY PRESS

Great Clarendon Street, Oxford OX2 6DP
United Kingdom

Oxford University Press is a department of the University of Oxford.
It furthers the University's objective of excellence in research, scholarship,
and education by publishing worldwide. Oxford is a registered trade mark of
Oxford University Press in the UK and in certain other countries

First published 2002
Reissued 2012
Reprinted 2013

British Library Cataloguing in Publication Data
Data available

Library of Congress Cataloging in Publication Data
Data available

ISBN 978-0-19-871174-2

In memory of Satish Loomba and Satish Dhawan, who were committed to building a humane and thinking society.

Acknowledgements

This book has gathered many debts. For inviting me to contribute to the series, and for their comments, I am grateful to Peter Holland and Stanley Wells. Frances Whistler at OUP has been extremely helpful throughout. Mary Worthington's work on the manuscript was invaluable. An Award from the Center for Advanced Study at the University of Illinois (Urbana-Champaign) gave me the much-needed time to complete the book. Support from the Research Board at UIUC facilitated the bulk of the writing. Over the past two and a half years, Lisa Lampert has shared her work, conversations, and a wealth of materials with me, and has commented on my draft chapters. I would also like to thank Joshua Eckhardt and Kimberley Woosley for helping me locate materials, and for their critical inputs into this project. For intellectual exchange and other forms of support I am grateful to Gifty Ako-Adounovo, Jonathan Burton, Dympna Callaghan, Peter Erickson, Jean E. Howard, Sujata Iyengar, Carol Neely, Patricia Parker, Daniel J. Vitkus, Charles Wright, Nina Baym, and Sanjay Kak. Rukun Advani generously and skilfully helped me race against time. Tariq Thachil helped me restructure the opening sections, and added serious conversations to his love and care. My communities in Delhi and Champaign sustained me in a period of transition, especially Zohreh Sullivan who made the prairie feel like home. Suvir Kaul has encouraged me, read drafts, and made home the most exciting place.

Contents

List of Illustrations

A Note on Texts

All quotations from Shakespeare are taken from the *Complete Works of William Shakespeare*, ed. Stanley Wells and Gary Taylor (Oxford, 1986). Spellings of all quotations from older texts have been modernized throughout.

Race and Colonialism in the Study of Shakespeare

Then and now

I imposed myself upon the world which was rejecting me, challenging their attitude against the colour of my skin, which they held up to my face as an exhibit of the stain against my person; I qualified the challenge with the submission that the quality of service I was performing the State cannot continue to be ignored, that it more than adequately compensated for the 'vices in my blood'. I argued the case that my worth cries out for recognition, even in place of acceptance, as it was said that Othello was respected and recognised but not accepted into Venetian society...I wanted to run because there was no such thing as a normal existence for the children of Ham.[1]

Thus writes Bloke Modisane, in his autobiography, *Blame Me on History*. Modisane grew up in South Africa, where a black majority was oppressed by a white minority, a situation that is practically the opposite of the one portrayed in Shakespeare's *Othello*, where Venice is an all-white city and Othello the only black man. However, 400 years after Shakespeare's play was written, Modisane found in *Othello* a mirror for his own oppression, as well as for his own determination to fight the racism of the South African apartheid state. During the same years and later, the so-called Renaissance was being taught without any sense that issues of race and colonial difference were central to the culture of the period. The novelist Michelle Cliff writes that she 'studied the Renaissance without dealing with the fact that the slave trade began in the Renaissance and that there were slaves in Europe even as Michelangelo was painting the Sistine ceiling. I was not even aware of it.'[2]

While Modisane took it for granted that Othello was, like him, a black man in a racist society, Shakespearian critics have been more divided, both about Othello's colour, and about its meaning in Shakespeare's day. Until fairly recently, many believed that Shakespeare had never seen a black man, and therefore must have intended Othello to be 'tawny' rather than a 'Negro'. Today, the fact of Othello's blackness is less contentious, but its meaning in early modern English culture still is. Some scholars suggest that blackness was viewed as the ultimate sign of degradation, while others argue that it began to be viewed negatively only later, as a result of colonial domination of Africans. They also differ about whether blackness was understood at that time to be a superficial quality, literally skin-deep, or as a sign of inner traits, which could not be changed. It has also been suggested that it may be particularly anachronistic to speak of racial difference in that period because whereas today the term 'race' carries overwhelming connotations of skin colour, in early modern Europe the bitterest conflicts between European Christians and others had to do with religion. As we begin to historicize these ideas, the question also arises whether our contemporary vocabularies are at all adequate for analysing the past. Are words such as 'race' or 'racism', 'xenophobia', 'ethnicity', or even 'nation' useful for looking at community identities in early modern Europe? Some of these words were coined only later and others, such as 'race', did not necessarily carry the meanings they now do. Even when we see modern-day meanings of words such as 'nation' or 'race' emerging in the early modern period, it is important to remember that older or competing meanings did not vanish overnight.

However, the fear of being anachronistic should not keep us from investigating the history of racial difference. Even today, race is a confusing term that does not carry a precise set of meanings, but becomes shorthand for various combinations of ethnic, geographic, cultural, class, and religious differences. While the colour issue is particularly prominent in the United States and to the history of slavery, anti-Jewish or anti-Arab prejudice has always turned on the question of religious or cultural difference. The conflicts in Rwanda between Tutsis and Hutus, or the caste wars in India, have not primarily centred on colour, but the victims in each case feel that they are racial in nature. A recent study published by the journal

Genome Research argues that 'the upper castes [in India] have a higher affinity to Europeans than to Asians, and the upper castes are significantly more similar to Europeans than are the lower castes'.[3] Colonial anthropology had suggested precisely this division, suggesting that the upper castes were 'Indo-Aryans' while the rest were a different race called the 'Dravidians'. Ironically, the *Genome Research* study would bolster the plea of the oppressed castes in India that the 2001 United Nations Conference Against Racism should discuss caste as a form of race. Their opponents insist that caste is *not* race because the former is social in nature whereas the latter is biological. This controversy reminds us that race is a highly malleable category which historically has been deployed to reinforce existing social hierarchies and create new ones. As Thomas Hahn puts it while discussing this problem in relation to medieval studies, 'If the elusiveness of race … equips the term to describe the complexity of modern social relations, it seems counterproductive to cite these same capacities (its versatility, its ambiguity) as reasons to exclude race from the analysis of medieval documents and events.'[4]

Precisely those visible features which are most commonly taken as evidence of racial difference (such as skin colour), are the most fragile from an evolutionary standpoint, which is to say that they are the quickest to mutate as a result of any sexual intermingling. Perhaps that is why skin colour produced so much anxiety in Shakespeare's time: the assertion that it signified a deeper human essence was always challenged by its uncanny ability either to vanish or to show up in unwelcome ways. If human beings were to be sorted into groups on the basis of shared internal characteristics, writes Jared Diamond, we would get groupings that contradict the ones that are commonly understood as 'racial'. Thus, for example, if the absence or presence of the sickle-cell gene that confers resistance to malaria was taken as a marker of difference, 'we'd place Yemenites, Greeks, New Guineans, Thai and Dinkas in one "race", Norwegians and several black African peoples in another'.[5] And the gene for lactose intolerance would produce different groups that still would not correspond to the usual visual markers understood as racial. In other words, what we call race does not indicate natural or biological divisions so much as social divisions which are characterized as if they were natural or biological. That is why the word is often put within quote marks today.

To say that race is socially constructed is not to imply that it is a delusion; 'false' as they may be, ideas about race have nevertheless had very real effects on people's lives. For that reason, I have not placed the word within quote marks, except when I focus on the term itself. We can de-naturalize ideologies of race but also acknowledge their continuing power by tracing their histories and showing how they have changed as well as solidified over time. Literary texts are particularly valuable in this regard, because they not only reflect and shape their immediate present, but also encode ideas from the past and visualize the future. Through them we can grasp the dynamism and flow of particular ideas and see how they are both transmitted and challenged. As we trace the history of race, particularly as it animates literature, we get a sense of not just the distance, but also the very powerful connections, between 'then' and 'now'.

Differences between various religions, languages, skin colours, and family arrangements were fascinating to European royalty, colonists, merchants, intellectuals, writers, readers, and playgoers, as is evident from the hundreds of books, pamphlets, sermons, and performances of the early modern period which focused upon these issues. The question of difference had previously been central to the literature generated by the Crusades and by the encounters between Jews, Christians, and Muslims in Europe. In Shakespeare's day, as Europeans searched for new markets and colonies abroad, they became culturally more open, and yet in many ways more insular. They began to bring in foreign slaves, and to trade with outsiders, but also to expel those they considered 'foreign' from within their own nations. They became increasingly aware of the power, wealth, and learning of other peoples, of the precise histories and geographies of worlds beyond Europe, and yet this awareness often only intensified expressions of European and Christian superiority. The debates about religious, cultural, and bodily difference generated during this period were profoundly to shape the development of racial thinking over the next 400 years.

Shakespeare's plays give us a sense of this simultaneous opening and closing of the European world. Through these plays, we can understand both the gaps and the overlaps between 'his' vocabulary and ours. Often, it is these plays which form a bridge between the past and us: even as we read in them stories of a bygone world, we also continually reinterpret these stories to make sense of our own worlds. Thus, Shakespeare has shaped the views of readers across many cultures and ages on questions of racial and colonial difference; conversely these readers' experiences of racial tension have shaped their responses to the plays. Of course, these views and experiences have been widely divergent—to some people, like Octavio Mannoni, Caliban's inferiority to Prospero in *The Tempest* confirmed that there is a natural inequality between human beings which justifies colonialism. To others, such as Aimé Césaire, the play conveyed the miseries of colonial oppression. Both Mannoni and Césaire not only claimed to have got their ideas from Shakespeare, but they also used Shakespeare to broadcast their views to others. Thus Shakespeare's plays have been an extraordinarily powerful medium between generations and cultures, a conduit for transmitting and shaping ideas about colonialism and race.

It is true that those who, like Modisane or Césaire, reach out across histories and cultures to make Shakespeare their own often do so by ignoring some very real differences between Shakespeare's times and ours. But, as the Caribbean novelist George Lamming pointed out, if his reading of *The Tempest* as a play that celebrates Caliban was a mistake, it was 'a mistake, lived and felt by millions of men like me'.[6] These responses remind us that beyond critical battles, plays like *Othello* and *The Tempest* have spoken about race to an audience whose lives have been, and continue to be, enormously affected by the racial question. As we strive towards a future where racial thinking has less destructive power in our lives, it is enabling to find a past where it had not yet acquired that power. For that reason, as much as in the interest of historical accuracy, many scholars want to find an early modern Europe free of highly calcified notions of race. And for others, the early modern period, or the medieval period, or indeed the classical age before that must be preserved as golden ages where racial issues were simply absent. It is as necessary to confront the long histories of race as it is to show that racial thinking has a history and is not a fixed or universal. The early modern period affords glimpses of other ways of being, some more flexible and generous, others more restrictive, than our own. *Shakespeare, Race, and Colonialism* will examine both of these, placing the racial question in Shakespeare's plays alongside some of the other writings with which they converse.

There are three broad 'streams' of ideas that go into the making of beliefs and debates about 'otherness' or 'race' in early modern Europe, and the vocabularies available to Shakespeare. The first is comprised of medieval as well as classical notions about skin colour, religion, and community. Greek and Roman literatures, Christian religious thought, as well as medieval writings, were influential in their views of cultural, ethnic, and linguistic difference. These views had been shaped by various histories of contact and conflict, the most important of which were the Greek and Roman interactions with the people they conquered, the Crusades, as well as the interactions between Jews, Muslims, and Christians within Europe, especially Iberia.

These older ideas percolated down to early modern times, but never in any pure form. They were constantly channelled through newer notions of otherness thrown up by more recent cross-cultural encounters, which we can think of as a second stream of ideas. During Shakespeare's lifetime, contact with outsiders became more attractive as well as more threatening for Europeans. First Spain and Portugal, and then various other nations, realized the potential of overseas trade and colonization. The fast-expanding Turkish Empire recharged older memories of the Muslim enemy of the Crusades, but it also provided a model for Europe's own imperial ambitions. The New World and its inhabitants generated a very different set of ideas about 'others' as either innocent or wild savages in a world of uncivilized plenty, ripe for European plucking. The newer contact with Africa made this picture even more complex, playing upon medieval notions of blackness but aligning them with the newer colonial promise of wealth and slaves. These histories of contact shaped the fate of those peoples within or nearer home who were never considered insiders—such as the Irish, the Jews, or the Moors—and vice versa.

Finally, in every society there also exist notions of difference between men and women, rich and poor, nobility and ordinary folk. Concepts of gender, class, and national difference have a profound effect on how any culture understands its own boundaries and can be thought of as a third stream of ideas, just as important for understanding 'race' as other histories of contact. Take, for example, the concept of the 'blue blood' of the nobility. This phrase is a translation of the Spanish *sangre azul*, which was claimed by several aristocratic families who declared they had never been contaminated by Moorish or Jewish blood, and hence had fair skins through which their blue blood could be seen. Thus blue blood is closely related to the idea of racial purity or *limpieza de sangre* which developed as the Inquisition sought to identify 'pure' Christians as opposed to those who had been 'contaminated' by mixing with Jews and Moors, or 'New Christians' who were converted Moors and Jews. All over Europe, the nobility were often understood as a 'race' distinct from ordinary folk, and colonial relations drew heavily upon pre-existing notions of class difference, although they also restructured the relationships between classes within Europe. In analogous ways gender difference was equally crucial to the development of race as a concept. Racial difference was imagined in terms of an inversion or distortion of 'normal' gender roles and sexual behaviour—Jewish men were said to menstruate, Muslim men to be sodomites, Egyptian women to stand up while urinating, and witches and Amazons to be kin to cannibals. Patriarchal domination and gender inequality provided a model for establishing (and were themselves reinforced by) racial hierarchies and colonial domination.

In practice, it is impossible to separate these three streams of ideas and histories as they mingle together to create ideologies of 'difference' in early modern England. In this book, we will locate how such mingling works in some of Shakespeare's plays, as well as in the culture at large. It is beyond the scope of this volume to consider every kind of difference, or every group who was considered alien or foreign. Nor is it possible to examine every Shakespearian play in equal detail. But by taking representative texts and histories, we can trace how vocabularies of race draw upon a whole range of ideas about skin colour, location, religion, rank, and gender, and also how they leaven older tropes with recent images and ideas, and learned ideas with popular beliefs. In this way, I hope to convey a sense of the historical, geographical, and social 'layering' of racial ideas and languages; we can then decide the extent to which Shakespeare drew upon, contributed to, or departed from them.

Insiders and Outsiders

Shakespeare's theatre, itself called 'The Globe', was enormously influential in forming English public opinion about the world.

According to the Swiss visitor Thomas Platter, 'the English pass their time, learning at the play what is happening abroad . . . since for the most part the English do not much use to travel, but prefer to learn of foreign matters and take their pleasures at home'.[7] By 1600, eighteen to twenty thousand visits were made each week to London playhouses. The bulk of these visitors got their images of foreign people from the stage, rather than from books or from real-life interactions. Thus the theatre deeply shaped English imagining of outsiders.

Our relationship to Shakespeare's theatre is analogous to that theatre's relationship to the outsiders it portrays. We find in Shakespeare's plays both the seeds of many of our own assumptions and institutions, as well as enormous differences between our own world and Shakespeare's. Similarly, the plays locate both an alienness and a disturbing familiarity in the many 'outsiders' they insistently portray. Indians, gypsies, Jews, Ethiopians, Moroccans, Turks, Moors, 'savages', the 'wild Irish', the 'uncivil Tartars', as well as non-English Europeans, were repeatedly conjured up on public as well as private stages. Sometimes such outsiders occupied the centre-stage, as in Shakespeare's *Othello* and *The Merchant of Venice*, or Christopher Marlowe's *The Jew of Malta*. At other times, they played smaller roles, like Aaron in Shakespeare's *Titus Andronicus* or Portia's suitor the 'tawny Moor' Prince of Morocco in *The Merchant of Venice*. Some were just shadowy presences that were evoked but never appeared on stage such as the 'lovely boy stol'n from an Indian king' over whom Titania and Oberon fight in *A Midsummer's Night's Dream* or the pregnant black Moor mentioned by Lancelot in *The Merchant of Venice*. Others are only figures of speech in Shakespearian drama, conjured up to establish a point of view: in *Much Ado About Nothing*, for example, Claudio affirms his decision to marry Leonato's niece whom he has not seen by declaring, 'I'll hold my mind, were she an Ethiope' (5.4.38).

For many years influential critics regarded such figures as mere footnotes to a theatre that was seen as predominantly European in its focus and interest. But, in fact, they help us scrutinize the very boundary between European and non-European, and see how it is constructed at a time when Europe's interactions with other worlds were becoming increasingly complicated. *The Notable History of*

Saracens (1575) compares its descriptions of the Muslims to the images reflected back by a mirror:

Here as in a mirror is set down, how, when and by whom, this pestilent generation was first set abroad, what success in their affairs ever since they have had, and if we will not by others harms take warning, what courtesy is to be looked for at their hands, when and wheresoever they can spy any occasion or opportunity to put in practice their bloody tyranny.[8]

The mirror image is a telling one: the past misdeeds of the Muslims are intended to warn Christians about the threat they pose again to Europe, and yet if they are set down 'as in a mirror' they also reflect the self-image of the Christians.

The work of Michel Foucault and Jacques Lacan (as well as other twentieth-century theorists) suggested that there is an intricate symbiosis between that which is demarcated as the 'self' and that which is excluded as deviant, strange, or 'other'. In his influential book *Orientalism*, Edward Said used such insights to analyse European attitudes to outside cultures. Europe's self-definition as the most superior civilization of the world depended in part upon the construction of an 'Orient' as different from itself, as an irrational, backward, lazy, sensuous, and deviant region.[9] The Orient was represented as Europe's 'other', and the difference between the two was crucial to sustaining Europe's image of itself. Such perspectives have revitalized the study of Shakespearian and other early modern representations of 'race' and 'outsideness'. According to Liah Greenfeld, sixteenth-century England was the first country in Europe to become a nation in the modern sense: 'a whole new class of people emerged whose main preoccupation was to do research and write—chronicles, treatises, poems, novels and plays—in English about England... Everything English became an object of attention and nourished a new feeling of national pride.'[10] Recent criticism has persuasively demonstrated that 'everything English' could only be defined by establishing what lay outside.

Suggesting that 'Self-fashioning is achieved in relation to something perceived as alien, strange or hostile', Stephen Greenblatt has shown how Renaissance aristocratic and upper classes fashioned their identities at least partly against the images of the newly discovered 'natives' of the New World.[11] Kim Hall has traced depictions of blackness in English poetry, plays, masques, paintings, jewellery, and travel writings that reveal a growing obsession with defining a white English self.[12] Descriptions of African or Turkish 'tribades' or women who had sex with other women, Valerie Traub suggests, fed into condemnations of same-gender eroticism in England.[13] Bringing the notion of 'other' closer home, Andrew Hadfield and Willy Maley argue that the development of 'Englishness' depended on the negation of 'Irishness' which was described as incivility, filth, and backwardness.[14] And James Shapiro identifies a similar dialectic in the relationship between early modern English culture and Jews.[15] Thus, although in numerical terms there were few Turks, or Africans, or Jews in England, representations of them are crucial for understanding the culture as a whole and its changing relationship with the rest of the world. Of course, the English differentiated themselves not only from the New World 'savages' or dark-skinned Africans, but also from Iberian Catholics. New and wider contact with Asia, Africa, and America helped to consolidate a pan-European, Christian identity but, at the same time, it also fuelled intense rivalry between different European countries for economic and colonial advantage in these foreign lands.

At the height of Britain's overseas empire, Rudyard Kipling suggested that it could not be understood in isolation from its colonies: 'What do they know of England, who only England know?' In Shakespeare's time, England had not yet become an imperial power, but it too cannot be understood without looking at what lay beyond its real and imagined margins. Having said this, we should be careful not to read descriptions of the 'other' as *only* a way of defining the 'self', because that would collapse all studies of difference back onto the dominant culture. In this period, descriptions of outsiders helped to shape actual interactions with them, to institute patterns of diplomacy, trade, colonization, and enslavement. Over time, they helped Christian Europe to achieve its historical dominance over other peoples. Images of blackness, for example, did more than produce ideologies of whiteness—they also helped legitimize actual exploitation of black peoples and nations. Finally, while these images obviously reshaped and even distorted reality, they were not complete fabrications but created in response to a certain historical dynamic. Often we do not have access to the view from the other side, to the impressions and assessments of these so-called 'others' of Europe.

Often we do not know how to read them or care to do so. But at the very least the idea of the mirror image should not be taken so literally that we see only Europe in European descriptions of other people.

Colonialism and European Nationhood

In an influential book, Benedict Anderson suggested that modern nations were born with the passing of an older religious and feudal order, which relied on bonds that stretched across national frontiers.[16] European nobility intermarried regardless of their national or linguistic affiliations. The monarch of one country could also become the sovereign of another, as happened in 1603 when Elizabeth I died, and James VI of Scotland became the monarch (James I) of England, or earlier in 1580 when Philip II of Spain also became king of Portugal. This social arrangement also depended upon a pan-national religious community. Earlier, the Crusades had attempted to cement such an inter-national Christian community across Europe. Fucher of Chartres had written about the mix of languages and nations in the armies of the First Crusade, which included

French, Flemings, Frisians, Gauls, Allogroges, Lotharingians, Allemani, Bavarians, Normans, English, Scots, Aquitainians, Italians, Dacians, Apulians, Iberians, Bretons, Greeks and Armenians...If any Breton or Teuton wished to question me, I could neither understand nor answer. But we who were diverse in languages, nevertheless seemed to be brothers in the love of God and very close to being of one mind.[17]

According to Anderson, nation formation involves breaks with such an order and the creation of a different sort of 'imagined community' in which people across different classes are united within a more bounded geographical space, and identify with the same language. Although Anderson discusses post-eighteenth-century events, several recent writers have traced the emergence of a similar dynamic in Elizabethan England. Until 1534, when King Henry VIII broke with the Catholic Church, the religious head of England (the Pope) was not English at all. In the period between 1500 and 1650, concepts such as 'country', 'commonwealth', 'empire', and 'nation' changed their meaning and became synonymous, all of them meaning 'the sovereign people of England'.[18]

New communities need to be *imaginatively* projected in order to be realized, and one of the best-known evocations of England as a nation in Shakespeare's plays is spoken by a dying John of Gaunt, Duke of Lancaster, in *Richard II*, who celebrates and laments the imminent passing of

> This royal throne of kings, this sceptred isle,
> This earth of majesty, this seat of Mars,
> This other Eden, demi-paradise
>
> .   .   .   .   .
>
> This blessèd plot, this earth, this realm, this England.
>
> (2.1.40–50)

The historical John of Gaunt lived in the fourteenth century and had multiple European affiliations—a Spanish wife, one daughter married to the king of Portugal and another to a Spanish nobleman. Writing in the late sixteenth century, Shakespeare appropriates Gaunt as the mouthpiece of an English nationalist outlook which was still being forged. Like a wide range of other contemporary writings (legal, cartographic, historical, as well as literary), Shakespeare's plays imagined and debated the idea of an English nation, and thus shaped its very birth.

Travelogues were a particularly important medium in this context, for they took their readers through diverse alien landscapes, inviting them to view the unknown through the reassuring perspective of a familiar protagonist or narrator. Thus they helped define the boundary between the domestic and foreign. In Shakespeare's lifetime, travel narratives became an important English phenomenon; Richard Hakluyt's monumental collection of voyages, *Principal Navigations* (1589; 2nd edn. 1599), made available the writings of older travellers as well as newer voyagers; fables and maps; outlandish stories about 'men whose heads | Do grow beneath their shoulders' (*Othello*, 1.3.143–4) as well as precise lists of foreign commodities and currencies. Hakluyt reminded his countrymen that they had lagged behind other European nations in gathering the riches of the two Indies, and he ardently advocated English participation in both 'Eastern trade' and 'Western planting'. Earlier, Richard Eden's notable collection *The History of Travayle in the West and East Indies* (1577) had also pleaded for English expansion overseas. English readers were invited, in Hakluyt's pages (and later in the collections edited by Samuel Purchas) to look at the rest of the world from a shared perspective, to believe in their common investments in overseas travel, trade, and colonization, and to enjoy the prospect of their future global success.

However, England's colonial ventures were not the result of its having achieved a confident and secure national identity. Colonial ambitions are often generated by anxieties about national identity.[19] Colonization was seen as the cure for various English ills such as growing unemployment, criminality, and hunger, the result, many argued, of a rapidly expanding population on a small island. Eden and Hakluyt both suggested that by exporting idle men to the colonies England would be able to restore itself to health, reap profits, and also contain the growing might of Spain, whose colonial wealth threatened to make it a European superpower. Hakluyt described idle Englishmen as cannibals, and feared that if they were not rejuvenated by colonialism, the English would become 'man-eating savages similar to those which inhabit the Americas'.[20] It is true that English colonial and mercantile networks were established later than those of other nations—trade with Morocco began in 1551, the Muscovy Company was formed in 1555, the Turkey Company in 1581, and the East India Company in 1600. Settlement in the Americas did not begin until the early seventeenth century. But England became involved in the slave trade as early as 1555, and through the accounts of pirates and other adventurers, foreign wealth and territories had long begun to dazzle English imaginations. In 1587 Francis Drake captured the Portuguese ship *St Philip* as it was returning home from the East, and two years later Walter Ralegh captured the Spanish ship the *Madre de Dios*; his commander thanked God for revealing 'those secret trades and Indian riches, which hitherto had lay strangely hidden and cunningly concealed from us'.[21] Rivalry with Spain and the desire to partake of the spoils of both Indies thus fuelled a nationalist rhetoric and the pro-imperial as well as pro-mercantile arguments in England.

The spectacular profits made by the first voyages to the East confirmed the promises of older travel stories, and on 31 December 1600 the East India Company was set up with a capital of 50,000 pounds. Queen Elizabeth granted it monopoly of trade with the East 'for the honour of our nation, the welfare of the people, the increase of our navigation, and the advancement of lawful traffic to the benefit of the commonwealth'. By 1620, the company had trading stations in Sumatra, India, Japan, Java, Borneo, Malacca, Siam, and Malabar, among other places. Accounts of the New World, such as Walter Ralegh's 'Discovery of the large, rich and beautiful Empire of Guiana' also painted elaborate pictures of the fabled Inca wealth and assured English authorities that whoever conquered this new land, 'that Prince shall be Lord of more Gold, and of a more beautiful empire, and of more cities and people, than either the King of Spain, or the great Turk'.[22] Edmund Spenser described Ireland in almost identical terms as 'a most beautiful and sweet country as any is under heaven', so full of nature's bounties that 'if some princes in the world had them, they would soon hope to be lords of all the seas, and ere long of all the world'.[23]

In Shakespeare's *The Merry Wives of Windsor*, Falstaff describes one of the women he fancies as 'a region in Guiana, all gold and bounty' and announces his intentions to make simultaneous love to two women thus: 'They shall be my East and West Indies, and I will trade to them both' (1.3.59, 61–2). Like Falstaff, England also seized the opportunity to traffic in both regions, although its modus operandi in each was significantly different: in the East, the English struggled to establish trade but in the Americas, by the middle of the seventeenth century, the imperial hallmarks of settlement and dispossession, violence and plunder were already evident. By the turn of the century 'both the Indias, of Spice and Mine' (to use John Donne's words) had begun to flood England with new commodities—spices such as pepper and cloves, cloths such as certain kinds of silk, artefacts, plants such as tobacco, potato, tomatoes, and chillies, and animals such as elephants. In 1599, the Swiss traveller Thomas Platter described the house of one Mr Cope, 'a citizen of London who has spent much time in the Indies' as 'stuffed with queer foreign objects'.

Platter's long list included 'An African charm made of teeth', 'Beautiful Indian plumes', 'Ornaments and clothes from China', 'A curious Javanese costume', 'A felt cloak from Arabia', 'Shoes from many strange lands', 'The Turkish Emperor's golden seal', 'A Madonna made of Indian feathers', and 'A long narrow Indian canoe'. The fact that it also included 'Flying rhinoceros' or 'A round horn which had grown on an English woman's forehead' and other fantastic objects should not detract from its testimony that England was witnessing an unprecedented exposure to foreign ideas, images as well as material objects.[24]

Queen Elizabeth herself received Platter 'with a whole bird of paradise for panache, set forward on her head studded with costly jewels' (192). Platter also mentions that at Hampton Court hung 'a lively life-like portrait of the wild man and woman captured by Martin Frobisher, the English captain, on his voyage to the New World, brought back to England alive' (201). *The Tempest* refers to the exhibition of this 'Eskimo' couple in London: Trinculo remarks that even though the English 'will not give a doit to relieve a lame beggar, they will lay out ten to see a dead Indian' (2.2.31–3). Not all foreigners were helpless captives though. In August 1600, London welcomed an embassy from the court of the Moroccan Emperor 'Abd-el-Malik, and many 'turbaned Turks' stayed in the city for nearly six months.

London's population tripled in the years between 1520 and 1600. In the first half of the seventeenth century, 10,000 people migrated every year to London from other parts of the country. So it is hardly surprising that questions of difference should have been volatile in the city. The terms 'stranger' or 'alien' were employed for non-English Europeans as well as Africans and Jews, who numbered about 10,000 people by the time Shakespeare wrote plays such as *Othello*.[25] In addition there were people from Scotland, Ireland, and Wales, who were neither fully outsiders nor insiders. After James VI of Scotland became James I of England in 1603, he tried to ensure that Scottish subjects born after this date would be considered English subjects in England. The king's attempts to effect a union between England and Scotland met with resistance from the House of Commons.

Throughout the sixteenth and seventeenth centuries both nationalist feelings and hostility to outsiders increased. In 1517, there was a violent riot against foreign artisans resident in London; in the same year, a preacher had moved his audience to violence by proclaiming that the increase in English poverty was due to the influx of aliens, and that God had earmarked that land exclusively for Englishmen.[26] This riot was later represented in a play called *Sir Thomas More* (possibly performed in 1593–1601) to which Shakespeare is believed to have contributed, and which was censored by the Master of Revels for its graphic depiction of the violence. In 1551, about 500 citizens had demonstrated before the mayor of London, threatening to kill foreigners. In 1595, tradesmen rioted against 'strangers' in Southwark. Such hostile demonstrations were frequent, the result of growing anxieties about being engulfed by outsiders. This is the atmosphere in which England began its overseas mercantile and colonial ventures, and in which Shakespeare's plays about outsiders were written and staged.

However, the idea of national formation as an anxious, unstable, and always unfinished process should not lead us to underestimate the aggressive connections between imperial ambition and nation formation. It is not just a remarkable coincidence, for example, that Christopher Columbus secured the funding for his overseas travels in January 1492, the same month in which his monarchs Isabella and Ferdinand took over the Alhambra, the last Moorish palace in Granada. Isabella and Ferdinand were enthusiastic leaders of the Reconquista, or the Christian movement to repossess Spain from the Moors. Later that year, the monarchs ordered the expulsion of Jews from the country and ordered Moors either to convert to Christianity or leave. Thus the drive to overseas expansion and the desire to create a 'pure' national self were two sides of the same coin. Competition between European nations also shaped colonialism—a year later, in May 1493, a Papal Bull split the world in half, awarding the Eastern Hemisphere to Portugal, and the Western to Spain. Other national identities in Europe were also intricately interwoven with the rise of imperial ambition and racial thinking, although in a less spectacular form. Iberian appropriation of the world was unacceptable to other nations, who consolidated themselves partly by joining the scramble for non-European goods, markets, lands, and people. It is useful to think about the 'early modern' as the 'early colonial' because colonization and imperial ambitions were the midwives that assisted in the development of the European nations, and made possible what we now call modernity.

Emerging national/imperial identities in Europe could never be entirely pure, could never successfully erase the long histories of intermingling. When Isabella and Ferdinand entered the Alhambra to take the keys of the palace from Boabdil, the last Moorish king, they were dressed in Moorish clothes. Their triumphant identities could only be fashioned by appropriating their 'others'. The Moors themselves would be shortly forbidden from wearing their own clothes, or even from speaking Arabic, all over Spain. In feudal Europe, clothing was not a matter of personal choice but was legislated by those in power. Just as women were forbidden from wearing male attire, or peasants from wearing the dress of nobility, ethnic and religious boundaries were enforced through dress. In 1215, the Lateran Council had decreed that Jews in all Christian countries needed to wear a badge of identification. Isabella and Ferdinand's order that Jews and Moors should dress like Christians and melt into the pot was no expression of liberalism but part of an attempt to create a homogeneous Christian nation. It was to result not in integration, but in further waves of expulsion, and greater anxieties about the nature of human identity, culminating in the infamous 'blood laws' whereby the Inquisition attempted to probe ever deeper into human beings to identify who a true Christian might be. Thus, as the nations of Christian Europe initiated their attempts to conquer and shape other people in their own image, what we call modern racism was born.

Impersonations

All theatrical images of outsiders or foreigners (as indeed of women) were embodied during Shakespeare's time by white male actors. Such impersonations had a long tradition in England. Since the medieval period, blacking up was a central part of the representations of the grotesque, the evil, or the exotic. Mummers' plays, miracle plays, and morris dancing all involved blackening the faces of performers. In royal circles too, there was a sustained interest in the enactment of difference. In 1510, King Henry VIII and the Earl of Essex dressed themselves 'after Turkey fashion', their torchbearers and six ladies covering themselves with fine black lawn to appear 'like Moreskoes' or 'black Mores'.[27] Between the 1510 and the 1605 masques, there are at least six documented instances of courtiers appearing as blacks; most famously, Queen Anne herself appeared as one of the black daughters of the River Niger in Ben Jonson's The *Masque of Blackness* (1605). James I was especially fond of Jonson's masque *The Gypsies Metamorphosed* (1621) in which noblemen disguised themselves as gypsies. These images of difference did not always hinge around the question of colour—court entertainments regularly included Irish characters who were white but whose alienness was enacted through their costumes (notably the Irish mantle) and through accented speech.

While these spectacles involved the impersonation of outsiders by insiders, they also showed outsiders becoming insiders by being physically transformed (as in *The Masque of Blackness*) or by changing their political allegiance or faith (as in Jonson's *Irish Masque* in which Irish gentlemen shed their mantles to indicate their submission to the English monarch). In the theatre, the outsider is not safely 'outside' at all—like the older figure of the wild man, he or she threatens to cross over the boundaries of racial or ethnic or religious difference. Othello is not simply the alien who crosses over by marrying Desdemona; he is also the exotic outsider who alone is capable of defending Venice against the Turks. Shylock draws attention to the unstable divide between 'the merchant' and the 'Jew' in Venice, and his daughter's conversion to Christianity reminds the audience of the fragility as well as strength of the boundaries between communities. It has been suggested that the figure of the converted Jew on the Renaissance stage represents 'cultural change and a fluid sense of self that one could call "modern"'.[28] But representations of outsiders who willingly or forcibly mould themselves in the image of the dominant culture are much more than shorthand for an emerging 'modern' preoccupation with self-fashioning and mobility. They testify to the fact that the very concepts of social mobility and self-fashioning, indeed modernity itself, were profoundly shaped by encounters with outsiders, at home and abroad.

These encounters opened up possibilities of the material exchange of goods, which most English people were to regard as beneficial, and they also contributed to ideologies of English superiority. At the same time, such encounters also threatened to blur precisely those lines of demarcation which guaranteed both material and ideological benefit, and conjured up the possibility of a reverse traffic whereby English people would 'turn Turk' (to use an early modern term) or 'go native' (to use a later imperialist phrase). English traders and pirates often embraced Islam, English colonists in Ireland adopted local languages, manners, and customs, and English colonists in America, it was feared, would cross the bounds of civility. Theatrical images of converted Jews, Turks, blacks, and Indians, of Othellos and Calibans who must learn the languages of Venice and Milan, allay the fears of Englishmen going native. But they are not merely images of containment; rather, they encode the violence as well as malleability of early cross-cultural encounters.

The hardening of racial categories during this period, I have suggested, was accompanied by proliferating images of hybridities and cross-overs in the writings and theatre of the period. In a remarkable passage, a character called Irenius in Spenser's *A View of the Present State of Ireland* evokes the long history of multiple migrations of the Huns and the Vandals, and later the Moors, into Spain. Although the latter were driven out of Spain, he says, their intermarriages and 'mixture with the people of the land during their long continuance there . . . had left no pure drop of Spanish blood'. Irenius claims that he does not regard such mingling as negative, 'for I think there is no nation now in Christendom nor much further but is mingled and compounded with others. For it was a singular providence of God . . . to mingle nations so remote, miraculously to make, as it were, one blood and kindred of all people, and each to have knowledge of him.'[29] Coming as it does after Spenser's anxious evocation of the English who have 'degenerated' into the 'wild Irish', such a vision of global hybridity reminds us of the contradictions that beset contemporary discourses about 'difference'. All human beings were children of the same God, according to the Bible, and yet according to the same Bible, they were sorted out into servants and masters, the accursed and the blessed, the black and the white. Shakespeare's depictions of outsiders rest upon and amplify such contradictions, evoking both difference and its dissolution.

Ways of Seeing

This book is divided into six chapters. Chapter 1 discusses the way the word 'race' is used by Shakespeare and in his culture, and also points at ways it was *not* used. Such usage, or the lack of it, helps us trace early modern conceptions of race as well as the differences that culture considered important. Chapter 2 considers how beliefs about skin colour and religious identity come together to create changing notions of racial difference. The discussion here focuses on Islam and blackness, which were spectacularly and intricately connected in medieval as well as early modern writings. Religious concepts of community were challenged most powerfully by differences in skin colour, sparking off intense debates about the depths of religious identity as well as of blackness. Such questions, I believe, were the very nerve centre of changing views of race in the early modern period. From Chapter 3 on, the book turns to individual plays: *Titus Andronicus* in Chapter 3, *Othello* in Chapter 4, *Antony and Cleopatra* in Chapter 5, and *The Merchant of Venice* in Chapter 6. Each of these chapters takes up specific aspects of racial histories and vocabularies that are illuminated by that particular play. *Titus* allows us to see how contemporary views of blackness intersect with notions of deviant womanhood, while *Othello* complicates that perspective by inserting a religious dimension that is missing in the earlier play. By showing us how Shakespeare dramatizes the cultural anxieties aroused by both blackness and Islam, these two plays help us further unravel issues of race and religion discussed in Chapter 2. *Antony and Cleopatra* gives us a vantage point from which to view the way in which racial ideologies are 'layered'—the play reaches back to classical stories about empire and sexuality, and weaves them with contemporary anxieties about colonial contact as well as about the purity of English culture. Thus it highlights the way in which ideas about race and empire are articulated in vocabularies culled from different periods, vocabularies that both gather weight and are transformed as time goes on. *The Merchant of Venice* offers yet another perspective on race, being the only play in which Shakespeare brings together issues of commerce with those of race, and also the only play in which he focuses on Jewish difference. It allows us to re-examine the relationship between religion and race, but also to consider how these concepts are complicated by emergent capitalism and the colonial market.

These different perspectives, while enabled by particular plays, are not confined to them alone. Capitalism is important for understanding the way race is treated in all the plays, not just in *The Merchant of Venice*, just as not only *Antony and Cleopatra* but all the plays layer older and newer ideas of difference. When we put all these together, a more complex picture of racial difference emerges, a picture that is not smooth and polished, however, because beliefs and expressions about race are often highly contradictory and inconsistent. Every chapter considers how the representation of race in these plays hinges upon questions of gender and sexuality, and on miscegenation. Certain subjects, such as the Amazons, or the 'pure blood' laws, which haunt the discourse on race, are considered in several different places. Because each chapter will build on what has been discussed earlier, the book is best read sequentially.

The conclusion briefly revisits *The Tempest*, which for many readers is the play that most clearly dramatizes a colonial situation. Critics have identified the early modern colonization of the Americas as well as Ireland as its historical contexts, but the island where the action takes place seems to be located in the Mediterranean, and the play discusses Europe's relationship with Africa. In the early part of the twentieth century, the play was widely appropriated by anti-colonial artists and intellectuals in Africa and the Caribbean. Thus *The Tempest* is almost global in its sweep, allowing us to think about the networks, overlaps, and differences between histories of race and colonialism in different parts of the world. Regrettably, it has not been possible for this book to consider all the different places and peoples which were important to early modern colonialism and thinking on race. Scholars of early modern colonialism had for long privileged the New World, and interpreted the sudden and dramatic encounters between Europe and New World inhabitants as emblematic of sixteenth- and seventeenth-century inter-cultural contact and race relations. My aim has been to show that other, older histories are equally important, and this has limited my discussions of the New World and of Ireland. However, the concluding chapter will indicate that none of these histories and contexts is isolated from each other, nor should any of them be seen as more or less important than the others in unravelling the place of race in Shakespeare's plays and times.

Race is, and has always been, a highly volatile question, and our view of it depends at least partly on which aspect has been important to us in our own life and work. Because Shakespeare too is such wide territory, appropriated by so many different kinds of readers and audiences, any book on Shakespeare and race cannot aim to be 'comprehensive' or 'objective'. I can only hope that this one will help stimulate further thinking and discussion on these consequential issues.

The Vocabularies of Race

Shakespeare uses the word 'race' barely eighteen times; like most of his contemporaries, he usually finds other terms to convey differences of religion, ethnicity, nationality, and colour. Moreover, his usage often suggests meanings not usually associated with the term 'race' today. This chapter will examine some of the ways in which this word was inflected in Shakespeare's writing and in early modern times. As we shall see, its usage was both distinct from, and laid the ground for, later deployments of the word, and of the concept. But early modern ideas about racial difference that feed into the modern idea of race cannot be inferred only from the use of particular words. After all, a rose by any other word can smell as sweet! The real question is whether and in what form the concept of racial difference existed in Shakespeare's time. That is why this chapter will also consider historical and conceptual issues about racial ideologies that confront us as we move backwards in time.

Lineage

According to the *Oxford English Dictionary*, 'race' was first used in English by the Scottish poet William Dunbar in a poem called 'The Dance of the Seven Deadly Sins' (1508) where the followers of Envy included 'bakbyttaris of sundry races'.[1] Here the word means 'groups' but does not tell us much about what kind of groups these might be. John Florio's Italian–English dictionary of 1598, *A World of Words*, defined 'razza' or 'race' as 'a kind, a brood, a blood, a stock, a pedigree'.[2] And indeed the word 'race' was most commonly used in this sense, i.e. to denote familial groups and lineage. John Foxe's *Acts and Monuments* (1563) speaks of Abraham's lineage as 'the race and stock of Abraham'. The French writer Montaigne also uses the word 'race' to mean family: 'I have no name that is sufficiently my own. Of two that I have, one is common to my whole race, and indeed to others also. There is a family in Paris and one in Montpellier named Montaigne ...'.[3] Shakespeare contributes to its usage in this sense, as when Antony claims that his love for Cleopatra prevented him from 'getting' (begetting) a 'lawful Race' with his wife (3.13.107). Here we can detect two meanings that would become important to imperial usage of the term—that of a bloodline or heredity, and that of a *hierarchy* between different bloodlines. The 'race' sprung from Antony and his Roman wife is the result of a legal marriage but also lawful because purely Roman, whereas his children with his Egyptian mistress Cleopatra are bastards, and of mixed ethnicity.

The centrality of sexuality is evident in this deployment of 'race' as lineage, which often shows up in the context of horses. Edward Topsell's *The Historie of Four-Footed Beastes and Snakes* (1607) speaks of 'mares appointed for race', that is, for breeding.[4] In *The Merchant of Venice* Lorenzo refers to 'a wild and wanton herd | Or race of youthful and unhandled colts' (5.1.71–2) and in *Macbeth*, Duncan's horses are 'the minions (i.e. darlings) of their race' (2.4.15). In Topsell's book, various physical attributes of the horse's body—thighs, tail, bones, stomach, and colour—indicate its nobility and temperament, suggesting a connection between outer appearance and inner qualities. Topsell's book also begins to describe human beings in terms that have become familiar to us through later racist discourses. It pictures a baboon, a 'Satyre', and an 'Aegopithecus', with erect genitals, and locates such creatures in Ethiopia, and among 'Moors' and in India (4, 13). The book suggests that 'Men that have low and flat Nostrils are libidinous as Apes that attempt women, and having thick lips the upper hanging over the nether, they are deemed fools, like the lips of Asses and Apes' (4). While Topsell does not use the word 'race', he lays the basis of a comparison between apes and black people. By 1634, this connection was made explicit by Thomas Herbert, who had no doubt that Africans 'have no better predecessors than monkeys'.[5]

Another meaning of 'race' that derives from its association with lineage is 'root', as in Shakespeare's *The Winter's Tale* where the

Clown wants to buy 'a race or two of ginger' (4.3.46). In *The Faerie Queene*, Spenser uses the word to refer to plant species ('the vertuous race Rose' (5.1.1)). It could be used to indicate humankind as a whole (as in 'the whole race of mankind' in *Timon of Athens*, 4.1.40) or different sections of humanity, grouped according to divisions of family, class, gender, nation, religion, or morality.

Faith/Nation

The idea of race as a national grouping is expressed in Sir John Wynne's *History of the Gwydir Family* (1600) which speaks of the 'British race'.[6] Such usage reminds us that the nation is a racialized category, and that, in the early modern period, national boundaries were increasingly defined by identifying its people as a 'race', or as a group with a common heritage, bloodline, and religion. Contemporary works like William Camden's *Britannia* (1586) and Richard Verstegen's *Restitution of Decayed Intelligence* (1605) propagated the idea of the English as an Anglo-Saxon race, as well as a distinct national group.

But the concept of nation was further complicated by religion, which was perhaps the most crucial factor in the development of racial as well as national ideologies. Peter Heylyn's *Microcosmus* (1621) quotes a poem celebrating the Hungarian prince Mathius Corvinnus, who supposedly slew 50,000 Turks, as the 'glory of his race'.[7] In this poem, the Hungarian 'race' is defined in opposition to the Muslim Turks, and the difference between the two groups is primarily religious. It is also political, in the sense that each group lives in a different place and owes allegiance to a particular ruler. The Turks were frequently described as a 'race' but more often as a 'nation', and in early modern writings, the latter term was deployed more often than 'race' to describe ethnic, geographic as well as religious difference. However, the word 'nation' did not apply only to people living in a particular locale. Jews, for example, were called 'a perjurious, vagabond nation', a group defined in part by their *lack* of affiliation to any one place— 'in their own country [they] do live as aliens; a people scattered throughout the world'.[8] Shylock is perceived as an alien even in his city of residence, and in contemporary writings, such alienation was regarded as a result of Jewish attachment to their faith—Henry Blount speaks of the Jews as 'a race from all others so averse both in nature and in institutions, as glorying to single itself out of the rest of mankind'.[9] However, the word 'race' was not widely used in relation to Jews; Shakespeare does not use it even when the question of Jewish difference is his main concern—instead, he has Shylock refer to his 'tribe' and Jessica to her father's 'countrymen'.

The religious underpinnings of 'race' stretched back to the Crusades. During these religious wars, each side was composed of diverse peoples, and yet each was also understood as a distinct group—the Saracens were identified by their allegiance to Islam and the Franks by their belief in Christianity. Religion was seen to confer certain moral as well as physical traits: thus Christians regarded Saracens as not only unreliable but also 'dirty' and often represented them as literally black. Were these differences, stemming from faith but manifested in moral and physical ways, perceived to be permanent or fixed? The Crusades had resulted in some settlements of European Christians in Muslim lands, and contemporary writers noted an extraordinary intermingling in these settlements (which are regarded by some critics as early colonies):

For we who were Occidentals now have been made into Orientals. He who was a Roman or a Frank is now a Galilean, or an inhabitant of Palestine...We have already forgotten the places of our birth...Some have taken wives not merely of their own people, but Syrians, or Armenians, or even Saracens who have received the grace of baptism...Different languages, now made common, become known to both races, and faith unites those whose forefathers were strangers.[10]

Although linguistic difference was fundamental to the medieval conception of race, in this passage we see that each side or 'race' could admit an amalgam of different languages and nationalities.

Somewhat paradoxically, these cross-overs do not really erode religious difference, because of which this residence in alien lands and mixing with strange peoples and tongues were all undertaken in the first place. Some Muslims can become Christians, but Christians and Muslims remain two distinct groups; the divide between the two groups in Crusader settlements was so absolute that some commentators have called it 'apartheid'.[11] And yet, no matter how strong the overlaps appear to be, there is a fundamental difference between the racial imagination of apartheid, which viewed different peoples as different species to be rigidly, and if necessary, violently kept apart, and the Crusading imagination, which could accommodate, even celebrate, certain kinds of cross-overs. The passage above approvingly notes the conversions of foreign women to Christianity, reminding us that religious conversion was widely considered one way of vanquishing the enemy. Conversions of Jews and Muslims, it was believed, would catalyse Christianity's ultimate triumph over all humanity. Indeed, the conversion of a *fair* Saracen woman became a staple of literary texts from the Crusades onwards because it affirmed the attractiveness of the Christian patriarchal order, without threatening its whiteness.

Conversion presupposed that all human beings were, in the words of St Augustine, sprung from 'one protoplast... [that] if they are human, they are descended from Adam'. Such a belief in a common inheritance certainly meant that 'race' in a religious sense was more porous than the later colonial notion of races as genetically distinct species, which is why Robert Bartlett concludes that 'although it may seem that medieval racial thinking was just as biological as modern pseudoscientific racism, it had as inbuilt components the common descent of all human beings with, as a necessary corollary, the implication that races had developed over the course of time'.[12] However, as we will discuss a little later, in practice, the idea of a common descent was complicated by ideologies of bodily difference, and particularly by blackness. In fact, it was the question of conversion which catalysed the development of 'biological' ideas of race; as white Christians confronted the implications of being infiltrated by Jews, Muslims, and blacks, conversion became a highly volatile question, with a corresponding reduction in the expression of liberal theology.

The intermingling of 'race' and 'religion' strengthened the moral implications of the former term. In 1594, Richard Hooker asserted that the English were 'the people of God' and also the 'race of Christ'.[13] King James I's poem 'Lepanto', celebrating the Christian victory over Turks, pits 'a baptiz'd race' against the 'circumcised and turbaned Turks'; the latter phrase is famously echoed by Shakespeare's Othello as he stabs himself at the end of the play.[14] Later, Milton's *Paradise Lost* speaks of 'the Race | Of Satan' (referring to his daughter Sin and their incestuously-conceived son; X.385–6) suggesting also that ancient pre-Christian religions of Asia were inaugurated by Satan's followers after their expulsion from heaven. Thus alien religions and peoples are assimilated into, and explained by, the moral binaries and mythical time-line of Christianity. Whereas Milton associates the devil with religions such as the ancient Babylonian or Egyptian faiths that were no longer practised, in early modern cultures the two religions that were Christianity's closest rivals—Judaism and Islam—were treated as the handiwork of the devil. Religious and literary texts as well as popular culture depicted Muslims, Jews, and the devil as black. In medieval drama, figures of Vice or the Devil were often in blackface; Reginald Scot's *Discovery of Witchcraft* describes how St Margaret, queen of Scotland was visited by a devil in the shape of a black man; Scot himself pronounced that 'A damned soul may and doth take the shape of a black more'.[15] Such writings helped craft the lens through which Europeans were to view the black people they encountered abroad—thus, for example, Thomas Herbert was to declare after visiting Africa that the people there were 'Devilish savages' or 'Devils incarnate', a view that is articulated in both *Titus Andronicus* and *Othello*.[16]

Whereas the association of dark-skinned people with the devil is acknowledged as racist, it is frequently regarded as religious prejudice when it surfaces in the context of Jews and Muslims. As a result, religion is often excluded from considerations of race, thus reducing the latter to colour prejudice. But, as the next chapter will show, the two are actually very complexly intertwined in the early modern period, neither identical, nor ever quite separable from each other.

Gender and Sexuality

It is hardly surprising to find that the word 'race' is sometimes used to define women as a distinct group, as for example when Spenser speaks of a 'bounteous race | Of woman kind'.[17] Inasmuch as 'race' denotes a distinct social group whose physical difference corresponds to inner qualities, women and men were perhaps the first 'races' in society. Beyond the actual use of the word 'race' in relation to women, racial difference was routinely expressed in terms of gender and sexuality, and vice versa. These analogies were crucial to the development of racial as well as patriarchal structures and ways of thinking.

Even before full-scale colonization, the myth of the Amazons most flamboyantly and consistently fused the notion of deviant femininity with a remote geography. Like the Jews, Amazons were spoken of both as a 'nation' and as a 'race', but whereas Jews were regarded as dangerous because they were a wandering and alien presence in existing societies, Amazons were seen as threatening because they formed an alternative community rooted in their own kingdom.[18] The location of these 'mankind women' constantly shifted in tandem with the horizons of the known world. Herodotus placed them in Scythia, and other classical writers in India, as well as in parts of Europe considered remote or barbaric. William Painter's *The Palace of Pleasure* had suggested that they 'occupied and enjoyed a great part of Asia' (160). Marco Polo and Pigafetta located them in Africa and Columbus and Walter Ralegh in the Americas. Amazonian homelands always moved to occupy the space just beyond a European horizon, a fantastic or actual locale that symbolized uncharted territories (Fig. 1). Like wild men, however, Amazons did not quietly inhabit their marginalities but threatened to spill out and aggressively overpower the world of (European) men.

Not only were Amazons located in faraway lands, but these lands themselves were often personified as Amazons—a sixteenth-century atlas, *Theatrum Orbis Terrarum*, described America as a woman who 'sacrifices | fattened and glutted men' cutting them up 'into quivering pieces' and either roasting them, or 'if ever the rudeness of hunger is more pressing | she eats their flesh raw and freshly killed . . .'.[19] Such descriptions made clear that such unruly lands needed to be contained, just as stories about Amazons hinged upon their domestication by Greek and other male heroes. The association of the Amazon with America, seen as a land of savagery and cannibalism, transformed the former from a figure who mutilated men into one who literally ate them. As we will discuss later, the myth of the Amazons helps us understand the construction of unruly, foreign women, such as Tamora and Cleopatra, in Shakespeare's plays. In literary as well as other writing of the period, non-European women are depicted as either dangerous (sometimes grotesque, sometimes very beautiful), and needing to be purged and annihilated, or alienated from their own society and made tractable, and therefore ready to be converted and assimilated into European family and society.

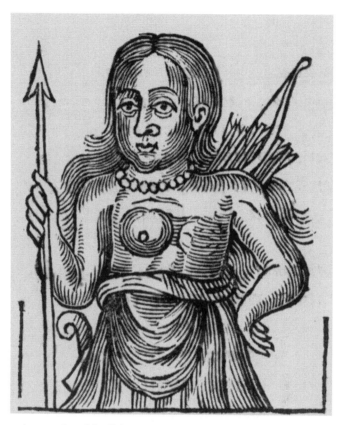

1. Amazon from John Bulwer, *Anthropometamorphoses.*

In early modern writing, not only are colonial lands sexualized, but sexual contact begins to be increasingly imagined as colonial possession, as in John Donne's 'To his Mistris going to Bed', where the poet describes his mistress as 'my America! my new-found-land | My kingdom, safeliest when with one man man'd'. In Shakespeare's plays, desirable women are repeatedly identified with colonial or mercantile spaces. In *All is True (Henry VIII)*, the queen is compared to 'all the Indies' (4.1.45) and Sir Toby compliments Maria by calling her 'my metal of India' (*Twelfth Night*, 2.5.12). Desire itself is figured as a mercantile or colonial relation. Troilus becomes 'the merchant' yearning for the unattainable Cressida whose 'bed is India; there she lies, a pearl' (*Troilus and Cressida*, 1.1.100). In Shakespeare's *The Merry Wives of Windsor*, Falstaff describes one of the women he fancies as 'a region in Guiana, all gold and bounty' (1.4.59). Thus European women are also assimilated into a colonial vocabulary.

In *The Comedy of Errors*, Dromio of Syracuse describes various bodily parts of Luce, Adriana's kitchen maid, in terms of different countries:

> ANTIPHOLUS OF SYRACUSE In what part of her body stands Ireland?
> DROMIO OF SYRACUSE Marry, sir, in her buttocks. I found out by the bogs.
> ANTIPHOLUS OF SYRACUSE Where Scotland?
> DROMIO OF SYRACUSE I found it in the barrenness, hard in the palm of her hand. . . .
> ANTIPHOLUS OF SYRACUSE Where America, the Indies?
> DROMIO OF SYRACUSE O, Sir, upon her nose, all o'er embellished with rubies, carbuncles, sapphires, declining their rich aspect to the hot breath of Spain, who sent whole armadas of carracks to be ballast at her nose.
>
> (3.2.118–41)

Here the descriptions serve to denigrate different countries as much as Luce's body; for example, the association of Ireland with Luce's buttocks echoes John Derricke's *The Image of Irelande* (1581) which described, as did other colonial accounts, Irish filth and savagery in anal terms.

Analogies between sexual and colonial contact worked to define both in terms of male possession. The two 'Indies' were repeatedly identified with female sexual parts, both in literary accounts, as in John's Donne's 'Love's Progress', where the lover sails towards his mistress's 'India', and in travel narratives, as in Columbus's statement that the earth was a breast with the Indies as its nipple, or in Walter Ralegh's statement that Guiana was a land that 'hath yet her Maidenhead'.[20] Hence, colonial space was sexualized, and women's bodies figured as colonies. But such heterosexual metaphors were disturbed by the fact that Europe, and England in particular, were also often personified as women. For example, appended to Ralegh's voyage was a poem by George Chapman, 'De Guiana', in which Guiana is pictured as an enormous Amazonian female who defers to her older sister, England. Moreover, the English colonial project was carried out in the name of a female monarch, Elizabeth I; Ralegh's 'Discovery of Guiana' ended by proclaiming that the Amazons 'shall hereby hear the name of a virgin, which is not only able to defend her own territories and her neighbours, but also to invade and conquer so great Empires and so far removed' (199). Thus the virgin Queen penetrates an Amazonian land.[21]

The strangeness of foreign lands and people was also expressed in terms of a departure from normative gender roles and sexual behaviour. Early modern accounts of foreign places and cultures, such as Peter Heylyn's *Microcosmus*, described the inhabitants of Africa as well as Asia as 'effeminate' (316). Such inversions haunt Shakespeare's Egypt in *Antony and Cleopatra*, where Antony is seen to be unmanned by Cleopatra. Muslims and Africans were also imagined as hyper-sexual and as given to same-sex practices. Travelogues, sermons, and other texts of the period described these practices in order to codify normative behaviour at home; of course, such accounts can be seen not just as a warning but also a fantasy, allowing writers and readers to savour scenarios of unusual sexual behaviour. But what I want to emphasize here is that during the early modern period, gender and sexuality provided a language for expressing and developing ideas about religious, geographic, and ultimately *racial* difference. European, Christian identity is increasingly expressed in terms of masculinity, its superiority and power are described and comprehended as the penetration, rape, or husbanding of an inferior and feminized race. In these accounts, the word 'race' is not always used, and the difference between Europeans and others indicated is not always regarded as immutable or absolute. But such difference is expressed both in terms of customs and language, and in terms of male and female bodies. Descriptions of the cannibalistic, naked American body, or the cruel or sodomitic male body and cloistered female body of Eastern empires that we find in the early modern period feed into perceptions of the New World as cultureless and savage, and the East as despotic, secretive, and degenerate.

We often speak of gender and race as 'mapping onto' one another, but, as we have seen, their relationship is more organic because one provides the conceptual framework for the other. When Europeans first ventured abroad, alien races were routinely described in terms that were commonly used to define women at home—as hyper-sexual, emotional, fickle, duplicitous, wild, jealous, and of inferior intelligence. But the comparisons always worked both ways, as in *The Winter's Tale*, where Leontes claims that women always lie, but then he strengthens his claim by comparing women's ability to do so to the falsity 'of o'er-dyed blacks' (1.2.134). Here, although the primary reference is to funeral clothes, the analogy serves to indict both blacks and women. Often, the comparisons are not made explicit, but embedded in the very language of gender and race: Dekker's play, *The Honest Whore* describes the 'honest' or reformed whore through the image of 'the Blackamore that by washing was turned white' (1.1.189).

With the advent of colonial science, analogies between women and 'inferior' races were used to pathologize both gender and racial difference, which is to say both kinds of difference were increasingly understood as rooted in biology, and as fixed. Both were often imagined in identical terms, such as a smaller brain for 'inferior' races and women.[22] In the early modern period, analogies between race and gender had already become important ways of defining each of these concepts. Finally, sexuality is central to the idea of 'race' understood as lineage, or a bloodline, because the idea of racial purity depends upon the strict control of lineage. In the early modern period, the term 'race' could indicate a family or household, a nation, a religion, a class, or even an imaginary group, but in every case, the boundaries of this group could only be guarded or expanded by carefully regulating sexual behaviour, especially that of women.

Class

In Shakespeare's *The Winter's Tale*, the young Princess Perdita and the Bohemian King Polixenes discuss the art of grafting or breeding flowers, 'an art which in their piedness shares | With great creating nature' (4.4.88–9). Perdita scorns grafting as artificial, but Polixenes suggests that sometimes nature itself allows for a species of grafting:

You see, sweet maid, we marry
A gentler scion to the wildest stock,
And make conceive a bark of baser kind
By bud of nobler race. This is an art
Which does mend nature—change it rather; but
The art itself is nature.

(4.4.92–7)

Here, Polixenes suggests that although inter-class marriages are artificial in that they 'mend' or act upon nature, they can also result in a pregnancy, which, being a natural phenomenon, breaks down the division between artifice and nature. Polixenes celebrates the happy effects of such 'grafting' because the union he visualizes is between a high-born son of 'noble race' and a woman of a lower social class, 'a bark of baser kind'. At this time (and indeed well into the nineteenth century), the father was regarded as genetically dominant, which is why Polixenes believes that the child resulting from such an inter-marriage would carry the imprint of his noble father rather than of the low-born mother. For the same reason, unions between high-born women and inferior men could not be looked at so favourably. In *The Tempest*, Caliban imagines that his coupling with Miranda will result in the peopling of the island with little Calibans, a scenario that is repugnant both to Miranda and to Prospero. None of them visualizes little Mirandas as the outcome.

In Polixenes' speech, 'nobler race' means 'nobler class' and it is striking that Polixenes conceives of each class as almost a different species. The word 'race' was most commonly used in relation to class identities—'noble race' or 'base race' are phrases that are ubiquitous in early modern English writing. In feudal societies, class was seen as an attribute rooted in the blood, or inherited, rather than an affiliation that can be acquired or shed. As discussed earlier, the phrase 'blue blood' evolved from the claims of Spanish nobility to racial purity; it not only defines a certain economic section of the people in terms of their skin colour, but also suggests that their characteristics are transmitted from parents to children. Peasants and lower classes were often regarded as biologically different from the upper classes, hence Polixenes imagines class difference as rooted in nature itself. Poorer people were widely perceived to be darker or more barbaric than their masters. Conversely, those whom the Europeans colonized were portrayed in terms that had already been applied to poor people—rude, uncultured, dirty, unrefined, and unintelligent. Noah's curse upon the descendants of his son Ham was popularly used to explain the servitude of European peasants, much before it became a rationalization of blackness.[23] Racially marginalized peoples were also described in terms of servitude, as in the expression that a Jew is 'a slave to the world'.[24] Another striking instance of the overlap is the supposition that both poor women and women belonging to 'uncivilized' races can give birth easily and without pain, and that labour comes naturally and easily to them. Poor women had long been understood to be hardier than their high-born counterparts, and in travel narratives, this idea crops up repeatedly in relation to native American women, Irish women, and African women.[25]

Polixenes' advocacy of an inter-class union does not need to be tested in *The Winter's Tale* because Perdita, whom Polixenes thinks is a 'low-born lass' or a shepherdess when he converses with her, turns out to be a princess. Her marriage with his son Florizel will not flout class barriers, or 'natural' divisions. In Caliban's case, on the other hand, several features of a class-based idea anticipate the inflexibility of colonial ideas of race. Caliban has several features attributed to the poor. He is ungrateful, incapable of learning, rude, rebellious, and physically repellent, a manual labourer, a 'slave' who aspires to unite with the princess. It is fitting that he teams up with the non-aristocratic Stephano and Trinculo. His difference or 'otherness' from Prospero and Miranda seems to involve both culture (he lacks their language, learning, and reason) and nature (he is biologically incapable of being improved and is physically distinctive). Miranda calls him,

> Abhorrèd slave,
> Which any print of goodness will not take,
> Being capable of all ill! I pitied thee,
> Took pains to make thee speak
>
> .   .   .   .   .   .
>
> But thy vile race,
> Though thou didst learn, had that in't which good natures
> Could not abide to be with.

(1.2.354–62)

Shakespeare's use of the word 'race' here indicates lineage, or inherited nature, which could apply to class just as easily as to race in the modern sense. However, the context in which it is uttered, an island which is hard to locate but which clearly indicates a colonial space, pushes the meaning of 'race' beyond lineage or class. 'This thing of darkness', as Prospero calls Caliban, is not just a displaced European manual labourer; in the colonial world, as we can see from Stephano and Trinculo's grandiose designs, even the under classes of Europe could imagine themselves as kings. These two also regard Caliban as monstrously alien, someone who smells like a fish; the first thought that comes to Trinculo is that he could be displayed for profit in England. Thus Caliban's 'vile race' indicates an amalgam of location, religion, culture, language, sexuality, and physique, all of which were part of the discourse of 'race' which was to remain volatile and variable in years to come. An undercurrent of violence was also to haunt the term, for no matter how genetically coded the concept became, the boundaries of race had always to be socially, and furiously, policed.

Colour

Shakespeare never uses the word 'race' in relation to blackness, which is significant given that, four centuries later, skin colour and race have become virtually synonymous. However, this does not mean that the term 'race' was never used in this way, or that blackness was not central to the development of race as an idea. The preface to Ben Jonson's well-known *Masque of Blackness* (1605) speaks of the 'Nigratae, now Negroes . . . the blackest *nation* of the world' but the masque itself opens with a song to 'Fair Niger. . . | With all his beauteous race | Who, though but black in face, Yet they are bright' (ll. 79–83).[26] The 'yet' here is weighty, and even as blackness is affirmed as beautiful, it is also confirmed as the crucial attribute of a particular race. Early modern writings increasingly use the word 'race' when they describe inhabitants of Africa, or refer to black people as the 'race of Ham'. Ham was Noah's son, and biblical and popular discourses widely suggested that God punished him for disobeying his father by making his descendants black in colour. *The Travels of Sir John Mandeville*, the most popular medieval travel book, had informed its readers that the inhabitants of Asia were descended from Ham (or Cham), Noah's disobedient son. Later, as Africa increased in importance for Europeans, Ham's progeny became associated with that continent. By the early modern period this idea was widespread: it is not black people's 'Seed, nor the heat of the Climate' that is responsible for their colour, writes George Sandys, because 'other Races' will not become black in hot climates, nor 'that Race in other soils grow to better complexion; but rather... the curse of Noah upon Cham'.[27]

In medieval culture (and earlier in Greek and Roman traditions) blackness was a symbol for a variety of differences. We've already remarked that the devil, the Saracens, and other enemies of Christianity were represented as black; so were Jews, allies of the feared Mongol emperors, or the Turks. Blackness represents danger, becomes a way of signifying what lies outside familiar or approved social, political, religious, and sexual structures. The stages of the early modern period were rife with images of black people as lewd, unprincipled, and evil, ugly, and repulsive.[28] These were not merely theatrical images: 'In our childhood,' writes Reginald Scot in his *Discovery of Witchcraft* (1584), 'our mothers maids have... terrified us with an ugly devil having hornes on his head, fire in his mouth, a tail in his breech, eyes like a bason, fangs like a dog, claws like a bear, a skin like a Niger, and a voice roaring like a lion.'[29]

In Shakespeare's lifetime, as English contact with sub-Saharan Africa increased and the slave trade proliferated, the associations of blackness and depravity became more widespread and intense. Conversely, the long association between blackness, on the one hand, and danger, immorality, sexuality, and faithlessness on the other, affected the way real dark-skinned people were viewed and treated. The question of skin colour was a vexed one in medieval as well as early modern writings—writers repeatedly debated the nature of the connection between skin colour and inner being, sometimes suggesting an overlap between blackness and immorality, and at other times affirming a disjuncture between the two. As we will later examine, they also disagreed about whether or not skin colour could change—Shakespeare's Aaron declaring that blackness cannot be 'washed white' and Jonson's masques dramatizing such a change. The important point is that the denigration of blackness as well as its praise, assertions of its fixity as well as of its mutability, all contributed to a racialization of skin colour.

Although Shakespeare does not yoke the words 'race' and 'black', his plays raise controversial questions about the social and moral nature of blackness: is it revolting or beautiful? What happens when it is introduced in a predominantly white culture? Does it signify a particular kind of inner being? What is its relationship with religion? Can a black person also be a good Christian? How does religious conversion affect blackness? What is the relationship between inner faith and outer body, particularly skin colour? Whiteness, as much as blackness, needs to be scrutinized when we think about the relationship between colour and race, because it too was constructed as an attribute of female beauty, or moral superiority, or religious purity.[30] In this book, I will concentrate on another aspect of the intersection between colour and race, and that is the relationship between religion and skin colour, which is particularly important for understanding changing views of race in the period. Through it we can grasp how the relationship between inner and outer being was viewed at that time.

Racism without Race

So far we've traced some of the ways in which the word 'race' was used or indeed not used in Shakespeare's time. We also need to reflect upon the concept itself. In an influential book, Robert Bartlett argues that in the medieval period 'the language of race—*gens*, *natio*, "blood", "stock" etc.—is biological' but 'its reality was almost entirely cultural'. In practice, races were defined more in social terms of customs, language and law, and all of these could be acquired or changed; pre-modern understandings of ethnic differentiation were less rigid than their later counterparts: 'When we study race relations in medieval Europe we are analysing the contact between various linguistic and cultural groups, not between breeding stocks.'[31]

Étienne Balibar goes back to early modern history in analysing present-day Europe, which, he says, is witnessing a kind of 'neo-racism' or a 'racism without race'. This form of racism, which is currently directed at (largely Muslim) immigrants into Europe 'does not have the pseudo-biological concept of race as its main driving force'.[32] It believes that Muslims are culturally, rather than biologically, different from Christians. Balibar suggests that such forms of racism can be traced back to the anti-Semitism of the early modern period.

But there is a crucial difference between Bartlett's reading of what 'cultural' (as opposed to 'biological') means and Balibar's. Bartlett suggests that because differences were seen as culturally derived in the medieval period, they were also more flexible, more bridgeable. Balibar makes quite the opposite point about contemporary neo-racism, one that is consequential for scholars of early modern Europe. He reminds us that 'biological or genetic naturalism is not the only means of naturalizing human beings and social affinities' and that 'culture can also function like a nature' (22). Culture can also function as an inflexible barrier.

If contemporary neo-racism is indeed like early modern anti-Semitism, then Balibar's comments alert us to the possibility that early modern racial thinking could be pernicious without being based on a fully 'biological' understanding of racial difference. Phobia about Arabs today, writes Balibar, 'carries with it an image of Islam as a "conception of the world" which is incompatible with Europeanness' (24). This assessment is borne out by much of the media coverage of Islam after the attacks on the World Trade Center and the Pentagon in the United States on 11 September, 2001. It is not dissimilar to early modern views of Islam and of the Turks, who were regarded as a real threat to Europe. Jewish difference too was seen as impossible to dissolve. Medieval and early modern Europe may not have developed a biological understanding of race, but in those deeply hierarchical societies, cultural change was unwelcome, at least to those in power. For example, Bartlett himself points out that English authorities forbade people of English descent living in Ireland from wearing Irish clothes or hairstyles, or from conversing among themselves in Irish. They were worried that by mixing with the Irish, the English race would become bastardized.

The rise of modern racism is often seen in terms of a shift from a cultural (and more benign) to a more biological (and inflexible) view of racial difference. But although the biological understanding of race made it more pernicious, we should be wary of positing a simple opposition between nature and culture or suggesting that a 'cultural' understanding of race is somehow benign or flexible. In fact, what we call 'race' and what we call 'culture' cannot be readily separated, especially during the early modern period when a 'people's inferior culture implied a biologically inferior people'.[33] Of course ideas about race did shift over time, and the early modern period is crucial for looking at those shifts. Some scholars have argued that the French writer Jean Bodin's influential treatise *Method for Easy Comprehension of History* (1565) marked a scholarly transition from a cultural to a biological meaning of race by suggesting that human characteristics are drawn from nature rather than from social institutions such as religion. Bodin used bodily characteristics, including colour, to sort human beings into four major groups: Scythian, German, African, and 'Middler'. Such examples however do not explain *why* racial feeling intensified at this time, or why, at a particular period of time, race began to be regarded as a biological condition. Some scholars date the 'new' racial vocabulary to the 'blood laws' promulgated by the Inquisition in early modern Spain, which tried to establish a correlation between religious affiliations and 'purity' of blood, between a 'cultural' category like religion and a 'biological' category like lineage.[34] Others argue that even before this time, Jews were regarded as a race, a group whose essential quality could not be changed by location, or even conversion to Christianity. We will return to this question later, but here I want to emphasize the fact that these changes in racial thinking were not just intellectual or theological developments but part of the power struggles in Europe as well as abroad. The blood laws intensified as Spanish Christians attempted to eliminate Moors and Jews and as Spain established its overseas empire and dominance over other groups in the New World.

In our own times, there is a tendency to regard racial thinking as simply a question of prejudices towards people not like ourselves. However, the history of race reminds us that prejudices are not just ignorance and bad faith, but help legitimize particular structures of power in which some people are deprived of their social, material, sexual, and intellectual rights.

Colonialism and Race

How did this connection between racial thinking and actual structures of power work in the early modern period? If early modern England was not yet a colonial power, isn't it simply wrong to locate in it the seeds of colonial discourses of 'race' or 'empire'? Should we not distinguish between the expressions of European superiority that we routinely find in literary and other texts of the period and the full-fledged racism expressed during the heyday of imperialism? Or remember that Europeans could not possibly feel equally superior to all the 'others' that they met—that if they could dismiss native Americans as cultureless, they could hardly do the same with the Turks, or Indians, or Chinese, or North Africans with whom they desperately wanted to trade?

The relationship between racial ideologies and colonialism is a complex one. While traffic in dark-skinned peoples and the colonization of their lands was to institutionalize and reshape colour prejudice on an unprecedented scale, crude negative stereotyping of black people (and especially black Africans) pre-dates systemic colonial slavery and exploitation, and in fact was used to justify slavery and colonial plunder. Moreover, not all histories of contact between Europeans and non-Europeans were identical, or had a similar relationship to emergent colonialism. Even though Americans, Turks, and Africans may each be described as a nation or a race, the settlements and violence of New World colonization reveal a very different dynamic from that of the trade and diplomacy with Asia. Whereas the Americas were 'discovered' by the Europeans in the fifteenth century, European contact with many Asian, Mediterranean, and North African lands goes back to ancient times, and thus their impact upon Europe was 'layered' rather than sudden.

These differences certainly affect contemporaneous discourses about 'race'. Early modern travelogues or plays of the period do not paint Turks and native Americans in identical ways. Turkish culture is seen as powerful and decadent, for example, whereas the native cultures of America are usually portrayed as primitive. The Turks are praised for their military strength and organization, or denigrated for their despotism and cruelty; Americans lauded for their simplicity or derided for their savagery. Cesare Vecellio's costume book of 1598 depicted an 'American' man as naked, with a tail, while its Turks were sumptuously clothed and arrayed. Very broadly speaking, inhabitants of Turkey, India, or Persia could be more readily seen by Europeans as peoples possessing their own histories and cultures, while native Americans were far more likely to be represented as unlettered, uncultured. These divisions were never watertight—thus the Irish could be seen as uncivilized, but their own poetry and cultural traditions could also be noted and regarded as dangerous. And Africans too were portrayed in contradictory ways, as wealthy and powerful (especially if they were Northern or Islamic Africans) but also as savages (especially if they were from sub-Saharan regions, particularly after the slave trade advanced).

These differences show up in Shakespeare's plays. Othello and Cleopatra are portrayed as royal, linguistically skilled, and proud of their long lineage whereas Caliban is close to the wild man of medieval tales, with a language that is unintelligible to others in the play, and with memories only of his mother. At the same time, there are also powerful similarities in the representations of these various outsiders. Sexual contact across races and cultures is scandalous: thus the actual or potential liaisons between Othello and Desdemona, Cleopatra and Antony, Caliban and Miranda, Claribel and the king of Tunis, Morocco and Portia, Launcelot and the Moorish woman, and Aaron and Tamora are all regarded with horror by several, if not all the characters in the plays. The plays, as well as travelogues and other writings, also often blur the specificity of different outsiders and versions of racial difference, or posit bizarre connections between them. For example, Samuel Purchas mentions the supposition that Jews come from the hills beyond China, and Holinshed writes that the Scots 'used at first the rites and manners of the Ægyptians from whence they came'.[35] Renaissance plays such as Marlowe's *The Jew of Malta* or Robert Daborne's *A Christian Turn'd Turk* repeatedly suggest an affinity between Jews and Turks. Categories such as 'Moor' or 'Indies' are often catchall terms indicating darkness or wealth—one contemporary writer points out about the term 'India': 'by that one name they express all wealthy (if remote) Countries'.[36] Thus, the literature of the period simultaneously distinguishes between the different 'others', and begins to encode a fundamental divide between Christian and non-Christian, Europeans and non-Europeans.

Colonial attitudes and behaviour also travelled from one context to another; English attitudes in America were shaped by their experiences in Ireland. Often the same individual colonists went out to both places.[37] Various English administrators such as Edmund Spenser, Sir John Davies, or Fynes Moryson describe the Irish as wild, thieving, lawless, blood-drinking, savage, barbarous, naked; these are also the terms routinely used to describe New World Indians. However, whereas Indians could be regarded as noble savages and some colonists could advocate treating them gently, the Irish were subjects of the English crown and had to be dealt with far more harshly because they existed 'within the boundaries of the state'.[38] Elizabethan writers also adopted the distinctions between civility and savagery that had developed alongside medieval conceptions about Ireland, writes Hadfield. Thus, ideologies of difference were both geographically and temporally mobile—the notion of outsiders honed in one part of the world not only influenced attitudes in another, but older habits of thought both reinforced and were themselves reshaped by newer histories of contact.

The process of racializing different peoples was a long slow one, and was not suddenly put into place by colonial contact. In the case of Ireland, a place that is often considered as England's first colony, Andrew Hadfield suggests that there was no significant difference between Elizabethan views and those that had been established several centuries earlier in Gerald's *Topographia Hibernica*, which proclaimed: 'The Irish are so barbarous that they cannot be said to have any culture . . . they go naked and unarmed into battle. . . . They are a wild and inhospitable people. They live on beasts only, and live like beasts . . .'.[39] I am not suggesting that there were no changes in attitudes to 'alien' people and the practices adopted in relation to them. On the contrary, writers in this period shaped new vocabularies and new ideologies of difference by using stories, images, and words from the past. Both positive and negative images contribute to the making of racial categories. Therefore, there is a complex rather than mechanical interrelation between ideologies of European/Christian/white superiority and colonial practices. Racial thinking developed and changed because of the new intermingling of attitudes to different kinds of outsiders. As we'll discuss later in this book, ideologies of skin colour complicated and hardened the concept of religious difference, just as fears about more recent immigrants such as gypsies intertwined with beliefs about Moors and Egyptians.

As we read the literary and other texts of Shakespeare's time, we can also find important, often uncanny, connections between early or nascent colonialism and a later imperialism. For example, in the nineteenth and twentieth centuries, the bodies of African subjects were displayed and dissected in order to 'prove' that their anatomies were different from those of the supposedly civilized races. One particularly infamous example is that of Saartje Baartman, a 25-year-old Khoikhoin woman who was exhibited all over Europe in the first decade of the nineteenth century and came to be known as the 'Hottentot Venus'. The Khoikhoin people of Southern Africa were pejoratively called 'Hottentots' by Dutch colonists. Relentless exploitation and genocide accompanied their exhibition as anthropological curiosities. Saartje's genitalia and buttocks were displayed as evidence of their pathological difference from those of white women. These practices were typical of so-called 'scientific' racism, but their seeds were sown in Shakespeare's time. Colonized people were already beginning to be put on display as objects, as we know from the reference to the display of a 'dead Indian' in *The Tempest*. The narrative of Martin Frobisher's voyage which captured an 'Eskimo' couple affirms that they were treated as little better than animals. In Cesare Vecellio's costume book we saw an American man depicted with a tail. As we know now, 'scientific' racism was not at all objective or scientific, and all early colonial representations were not simply ignorant or mythical.

In the heyday of imperialism, breasts of Khoikhoin and Khoisan women were used as pouches, as indeed were the breasts of native American women. Such a practice is recommended in John Bulwer's 1653 book *Anthropometamorphoses*, which suggests that the breasts of Irish women 'were fit to be made money bags for East or West-Indian Merchants, being more than half a yard long, and as well wrought as any Tanner with the like Charges could ever mollify such leather'.[40] The picture that accompanies these lines shows an Irish woman suckling her child with a breast that is thrown over her shoulder (Fig. 2). Precisely the same image of over-the-shoulder breast-feeding is also evoked in relation to native American and African women during this period. The idea that women of alien or monstrous races had enormous breasts goes back to ancient and medieval writers like Pliny the Elder and John Mandeville. In early modern Europe it was redeployed to sexualize the bodies of women from countries that were, or were about to be, colonized, and to suggest their animal-like savagery and difference from civilized women.[41] The distance between these earlier writings and those about 'Hottentot' women is not absolute.

2. Irish woman suckling her child from John Bulwer, *Anthropometamorphoses*.

Of course this does not mean that we should look back into the early modern past only to locate the roots of later racist thought—we also need to reach back to find other views of difference that were discarded over time, or which survived only as alternative perspectives. Shakespeare's plays bear traces of different attitudes to race, and allow us to trace debates and contests about it rather than only those opinions which became dominant as colonialism advanced.

Religion, Colour, and Racial Difference

Apart from Morocco, one of Portia's suitors in *The Merchant of Venice*, there are only two black men in Shakespeare's plays: Aaron, the evil Moor of *Titus Andronicus* (1593–4) and the valiant Moorish hero of *Othello* (1604). These two plays are usually juxtaposed only to highlight the enormous distance Shakespeare seems to have traversed in his understanding of the 'black Moor'. The difference between the two characters is not just that Aaron is pathologically evil whereas Othello is a more complex mix of nobility and violent jealousy, but that they highlight different aspects of the term 'Moor', a word that could mean both 'Muslim' and 'black'. Aaron's depravity is attributed entirely to his colour—he is repeatedly called 'irreligious' and boasts himself that he holds no God sacred. Although the play does not comment directly on his religion, 'valiant Othello', with his 'bombast circumstance | Horribly stuffed with epithets of war' (1.1.13–14), his 'sword of Spain' (5.2.260) and his violent jealousy, evokes Renaissance stereotypes of the 'malignant and a turbaned Turk' (5.2.362). Aaron leads us to literary, religious, and theatrical traditions that had equated black skin with godlessness and sin, and their relation with emergent colonialism. *Othello* invites us to consider how that lineage is also intertwined with the long history of Christian interactions with various kinds of Muslims—the Saracens of the Holy Crusades, the Arab Moors of Spain, the Turks whose growing empire threatened Europeans, as well as the Moroccans, Indians, and others with whom the English wanted to trade.

Together, these two histories illuminate how religion and skin colour intersect in the development of race as a concept. Until recently, religious prejudice was often distinguished much too drastically from racism, which meant that histories of Christian interactions with Jews and Muslims were neglected. Consequently, race became equated with colour prejudice. Even though scholars have now begun to consider the role of religion, the tendency to isolate it from or counter-pose it to questions of skin colour or bodily difference still persists. For example, as it becomes clear that *Othello* cannot be understood without understanding attitudes to Turks and Muslims, it is sometimes suggested that hatred and fear of Muslims was *more* important than colour prejudice in English culture. In my view, religion should not obscure or undermine the place of somatic difference; instead, we need to locate how the two come together and transform each other in the early modern period. This intersection also sheds light on the play of nature and culture in racial ideologies, which was briefly discussed in the previous chapter. Although the place of Jews is crucial to this process, it will be taken up more fully in Chapter 6; here (and over the next two chapters) we will focus more on Islam and blackness.

Although the word 'Moor' increasingly became associated with blackness, it first indicated those who belonged to 'Mahomet's sect'.[1] The people of mixed Arab and Berber ancestry and Islamic faith who came to Spain in the eighth century were called 'Moro' by those whom they conquered, but they were not necessarily dark-skinned. Both blackness and Islam had been the target of hatred as well as fascination in medieval Europe, but the sources of this antipathy were not necessarily identical. However, Islam and blackness were regarded as overlapping categories for Christians from the Crusades onwards. For Shakespeare's audiences, certainly, the word Moor was an amalgam of both religious and colour difference: *The Merchant of Venice* refers to the 'Moor' made pregnant by Launcelot as 'Negro' (3.5.37–8). According to Leo Africanus, Moors come in various colours, ranging from black and tawny to white. It has been suggested that in translating Africanus's writings into English, John Pory was the first to fuse blackness and Islam into the word Moor.[2] In English theatre, 'Moor' is primarily associated with blackness and 'Moorishness' is generally a set of attributes that cannot be either acquired or shed.

The association of godlessness and blackness goes back to medieval literature and theology, but it was increasingly reinforced by the slave trade. An account of John Lok's voyage to Guinea in 1555, which brought five captives into England, reported that the people who lived in Africa 'were in old time called Aethiopes and Nigritae, which we now call Moores, Moorens, or Negroes, a people of beastly living, *without a God, law, religion, or commonwealth*'.³ The view that many (especially sub-Saharan) Africans lived under no organized religion, and were 'of beastly living', circulated in many travelogues, including an influential account of Africa by Leo Africanus, a Spanish Muslim who had converted to Christianity.⁴ The coat of arms of John Hawkins, who took 300 captives from the Guinea coast to the West Indies in 1562, flaunted three shackled black men, and his crest depicted a bound Moor.⁵ The slave trade linked blackness to servitude, as well as to moral inferiority and ugliness.

In order to trace the relationship between blackness and Islam, let us turn to a text written 300 years before *Othello*. Early in the thirteenth-century Arthurian romance *Parzival*, there is a scene that is practically unimaginable in Renaissance drama. It is a romantic interlude between Gahmuret, a noble Arthurian knight, and a black Moorish queen: 'No one was present—the maidens had gone out and shut the door after them—and the queen bestowed a sweet and noble love, as did Gahmuret, her heart's beloved. Yet their skins were not alike in colour.'⁶ The love between Gahmuret and the black queen is 'noble' and 'true', and no one regards it as 'foul lust' which, in the literature of Shakespeare's times, becomes the dominant label attached to the desire between black women and white men. But Gahmuret cannot stay with the queen, not because she is black, but because she is not a Christian. He leaves her with a note saying that if she 'will receive baptism, you may yet win me back' (32). The lady mourns him, saying that if he were to return, 'I would gladly agree to be baptized and live as he desired'. Some time later, the black queen gives birth to 'a son who was of two colours and in whom God had wrought a marvel, for he was both black and white. Immediately the queen kissed him over and over again on his white spots... Like a magpie was the colour of his hair and of his skin' (32–3).

The story of the dappled child does not tell us that differences in skin colour were not important at that time, but rather that religious and cultural differences were already colour-coded. For Wolfram, the author of *Parzival*, 'black is the colour of hell, white the colour of heaven' (3). The black/white dichotomy fuses with the one between Islam and Christianity. For medieval writers and painters, Christian purity was symbolized by whiteness, and Islam marked a discoloration; therefore dark colour marked its followers, the Saracens. Love across the boundaries might threaten to erode these divisions but eventually it can only produce a literal embodiment of the tension between them.

Towards the end of *Parzival*, there is a pitched battle between 'a baptized man' and a 'heathen'. It turns out that 'the heathen' is the dappled child, Feirefiz, now grown to be a brave warrior, and 'the baptized man' is Parzival, son of Gahmuret by a white Christian woman. The author laments: 'I must mourn their fighting from loyalty of heart because one flesh and one blood are doing one another such harm. Both of them were after all, sons of one man' (386). When they realize they are half-brothers, Parzival and Feirefiz make much of each other. Later, Feirefiz falls in love with a beautiful lady, Repanse de Schoye, who bears the Holy Grail. However, since he is a heathen, he can neither see the Grail nor marry Repanse. Whereas Feirefiz's mother had made the mistake of retaining her religious identity, Feirefiz's love for Repanse spurs him to cross over to Christianity: '"Whatever I have to do to have the girl", said the heathen, "that I will do, and faithfully"' (425). We do not hear whether his baptism brings about a change in Feirefiz's complexion, but the others 'begin to treat him as a Christian' (426), the Holy Grail becomes miraculously visible to him, and he is allowed to marry Repanse and take her back to his country, which we are now told is India. There, Repanse gives birth to a child who grows up to be Prester John, a figure widely celebrated in contemporary literature as the white, Christian ruler of various faraway lands including India and Ethiopia. In *Parzival*, Feirefiz orders his son's 'writings to be sent all over the land of India about what Christian life was like. It had not been so strong there previously.' Repanse's brother Anfortas is pleased 'that his sister was now the uncontested mistress of many lands so vast' (428).

The themes of desire and difference, mirroring and conversion, religion and property that structure the intercultural relationships in this remarkable romance haunt literature three centuries later. But there are crucial differences between the two periods. In *Parzival*, Feirefiz the heathen and Parzival the holy knight can be imagined as half-brothers and as sharing a common knightly ethos. After his conversion, Feirefiz can be allowed to husband the noblest Christian maiden and father the legendary Prester John. This does not mean that in the thirteenth century the differences between Christian and heathen were regarded as entirely superficial. Feirefiz's dappled skin is a graphic reminder of the difficult distance between them. In some medieval texts, such as the *King of Tars* romance, conversion to Christianity often results in a literal whitening of the skin, or a shedding of bestial physical features, but we do not see that in *Parzival*. By the Renaissance, the literal transformation of the black body becomes much rarer, although we do see it represented on the stage by the miraculous whitening of the black daughters of the River Niger in Ben Jonson's *Masque of Blackness* (1605). Black women can rarely be portrayed as romantic partners of white men, although fair Muslim women repeatedly are. However, in early modern literature, questions of colour continue to be yoked with those of religious and cultural conversions, and as in *Parzival*, these conversions continue to hinge on romantic and sexual love.

Blacks

Different as Othello is from Aaron, neither can escape the charge of bestial sexuality. By the time Shakespeare was writing these plays, there had been a long tradition that equated blackness with lechery. An extraordinary Roman mosaic dating to the second century AD, found at the entrance to the public baths in Timgad (in present-day Algeria), depicts a bath attendant or person who shovelled coal into the furnaces for the heating of the baths as a black man with an enormous erect and dripping penis (Fig. 3). This figure provides a spectacular visual link between two Latin terms—'fornactor' (or one who stokes a furnace or 'fornax') and 'fornicator' (or one who indulges in sex or 'fornicatio', which derives from 'fornix' meaning a vault or arch, and also a vaulted space where prostitutes plied their trade). The two terms are etymologically connected because both furnaces and sexuality are associated with heat. In English, these connections

3. Black bath attendant in a Roman mosaic dated second century AD.

became even more explicit: the word 'fornicate', the *OED* tells us, means lechery as well as a space that is 'arched, vaulted like an over or furnace'. The association between furnaces and lechery in the figure of the bath attendant is established via his blackness; conversely, it reinforces the connections of blackness with literal as well as sexual heat. By the Renaissance, an association between blackness and forni-cation was widespread. Francis Bacon's *New Atlantis* claimed that

when 'an holy Hermit...desired to see the Spirit of Fornica-
tion...there appeared to him, a foule ugly Ethiope'.[7] John Bulwer's
Anthropometamorphoses repeated an idea that had become common—
that every man of Ham's 'race', including the 'Negro Pigmies who
dwell in the middle of India', has been punished with such a large
penis that 'it hangs down even to their Ankles'.[8]

Black people were also said to indulge in same-sex practices, and
even to couple with animals. Mandeville's *Travels* had described
'the Fiends of Hell' coupling with Babylonian women to produce
'Monsters'. Such stories now morphed into tales of sex between
non-Christian (and usually dark-skinned) peoples with animals.
Jean Bodin suggested that 'promiscuous coition of men and animals
took place, wherefore the regions of Africa produce for us so
many monsters'.[9] Iago plays with such ideas when he wakes up
Brabanzio with the news that his daughter has run away with
Othello:

> Even now, now, very now, an old black ram
> Is tupping your white ewe. Arise, arise!
> Awake the snorting citizens with the bell,
> Or else the devil will make a grandsire of you.
>
> (1.1.88–91)

Here, the black man does not couple with, but is identified as, animal
and devil. He is 'a Barbary horse' who will engender animals: 'you'll
have your nephews neigh to you, you'll have coursers for cousins and
jennets for germans' (1.1.114–15). In Iago's eyes and Brabanzio's,
Othello's coupling with Desdemona is just as unnatural as the supposed lust between animals and people in Africa. Brabanzio wonders
how his daughter 'could err | Against all rules of nature' (1.3.100–1).
Iago echoes this, telling Othello that Desdemona's refusal to accept
'matches | Of her own clime, complexion, and degree | Whereto we
see in all things nature tends' shows that she has 'a will most rank, |
Foul disproportions, thoughts unnatural!' (3.3.234–8).

In Jonson's *Volpone*, we hear that Volpone has coupled with
'beggars | gypsies and Jews and blackmoors' and produced monstrous
children—a dwarf, a fool, and a eunuch. The inclusion of 'beggars' in
the list reminds us that class differences also shape the category of the
monstrous or uncivilized. In *Titus Andronicus*, the liaison of white

Tamora and black Aaron produces a child who is repeatedly called a 'devil'. By bringing this baby on stage, Shakespeare was doing something entirely unprecedented, but it was also a scene he never repeated. Aaron's son is the only child of an interracial couple that we actually see on the early modern stage in England.

Like Spain and Portugal, England also became increasingly hostile and anxious about the presence of outsiders within its borders precisely at the same time as it sought to expand its own frontiers. Jews had been officially expelled as early as 1290. Both Queen Mary and Queen Elizabeth issued new proclamations against foreigners. In 1596 Elizabeth sent a letter to the mayors of London and other towns asking that black people be deported. A week later, Casper van Senden, a merchant from Lübeck, offered to arrange the release of eighty-nine English prisoners in Spain and Portugal in exchange for eighty-nine 'blackamoores' living in England who were to be handed over to him to be traded as slaves. The queen thought this 'a very good exchange and that those kinde of people may be well spared in this realme'. However, the land remained unpurged of blacks, for in 1601 Elizabeth proclaimed that she was

highly discontented to understand the great numbers of Negroes and black-amoors which (as she is informed) are carried into this realm since the troubles between her highness and the King of Spain; who are fostered and powered here, to the great annoyance of her own liege people that which co[vet?] the relief which these people consume, as also for that the most of them are infidels having no understanding of Christ or his Gospel: hath given a special commandment that the said kind of people should be with all speed avoided and discharged out of this her majesty's realms . . . [10]

Elizabeth's fear that 'blackamoors' were depriving Christians of food and employment demonstrates that the anxiety generated by them was disproportionate to the actual numbers of black people in the country. Her proclamation suggests that 'blackamoors' have come to England after being expelled from Spain. The expulsions of Moors and Jews from Spain produced complaints on both sides that these communities were relocating to England. If Elizabeth is indeed referring to Spanish 'Moors', it is significant that she should call them 'Negroes and blackamoores' because there was no major colour difference between Spanish Muslims and Christians. Elizabeth seems more annoyed by the fact of these people being 'infidels' than by their colour, but religious difference is, as we've seen, often expressed in terms of colour. While Iberian Jews and Moors were given only limited and rather fraught options to convert to Christianity, the 'Negroes and blackamoores' thrown out by Elizabeth were given none.

Theories of Blackness

The account of John Lok's voyage to Guinea which suggested that the people of Guinea lived under no organized religion or society also claimed that Moors were 'so scorched and vexed with the heat of the sun, that in many places they curse it when it riseth'. The belief that blackness was a result of hot climate goes back to the Roman writer Pliny's *Natural History* and surfaces in several of Shakespeare's plays. In *The Merchant of Venice*, Portia's suitor from Morocco says his complexion is the 'shadowed livery of the burnished sun' (2.1.2) while Cleopatra boasts that she is 'with Phoebus' amorous pinches black' (1.5.28). Many contemporary accounts argued that both 'diverse complexions of body' and different 'conditions of mind' were the result of 'diverse climates of the Earth':

> The Northern man is fair, the Southern foul
> That's white, this black, that smiles and this doth scowl . . . [11]

Here, variations in skin colour as well as temperament are explained by location. The theory of humours, derived from Greek medicine, suggested that different personalities result from various combinations of four 'humours' (from the Latin word for 'liquid' or 'fluid'). The four cardinal humours were blood, phlegm, choler (yellow bile), and melancholy (black bile), and it was believed that an excess of any of them would result in an unbalanced personality—hence excessive 'blood' would produce an excitable person, and excess of yellow bile would result in irritability. It is significant that humours were also believed to affect skin colour: yellow bile would produce a jaundiced temperament as well as yellow skin. 'Complexion' was originally another word for temperament, and its shift to a primarily somatic meaning can be related to the sharpening of colour-consciousness in Europe.

The humours were not understood to be permanently fixed, so that human 'complexion' was, in theory, constantly subject to change. But

the connection between temperament and location gave rise to stereotypes that became fixed as attributes of particular races. For example,
Robert Burton's influential *The Anatomy of Melancholy* suggests that
'Southern men are more hot, lascivious, and jealous, than such as
live in the North'.[12] Jealousy became widely understood as a trait of
Moors, Turks, and Africans, even if, like Othello, they no longer lived
in 'the South'. Therefore, although humoural and climatic theories
offered a more flexible view of human personality as well as skin colour
than did later racial theory, in practice such flexibility was not always
evident.

During Shakespeare's time the climatic theory of skin colour began
to be questioned. If some accounts of Lok's journey to Guinea suggested that Moors were 'scorched' by the sun, other accounts of the
same journey produced a counter-argument. One of the five captives
brought to England by Lok reportedly married an Englishwoman
who gave birth to a black child. The story was related with horror by
George Best's *A True Discourse of the Late Voyages of Discovery* (1578):

I my self have seen an Ethiopian as black as coal brought into England, who
taking a faire English woman to wife, begat a son in all respects as black as the
father was, although England were his native country, and an Englishwoman
his mother: whereby it seemeth this blackness proceedeth rather of some
natural inflection of that man, which was so strong, that neither the Clime,
neither the good complexion of the mother concurring, could anything alter.[13]

Here blackness is a 'natural inflection' unaffected by climate, and
powerful enough to override the white mother's complexion. Other
writers like Peter Heylyn pointed to the light skin of Americans to
argue against the connection between climate and colour:

The inhabitants (though a great part of this country lieth in the same parallel
with Ethiopia, Lybia and Numidia) are of reasonably fair complexion, and
very little (if at all) inclining to blackness. So that the extraordinary and
continual vicinity of the Sun, is not as some imagine the operative cause of
blackness: though it may much further such a colour, as we see in our country
lasses, whose faces are always exposed to wind and weather.[14]

Heylyn scoffs at the idea, first suggested by the Greek philosopher
Herodotus, that the 'generative feed' or semen of Africans is black,
concluding that skin colour is the result of 'God's peculiar will and
ordinance' (403).

Others offered a different kind of religious explanation. George Best's 'True Discourse', as we discussed in Chapter 1, explains blackness as the result of Ham's filial disobedience. Best suggested that the 'wicked Spirit' who caused Adam to sin also prompted Cham (or Ham) to disobey his father Noah's instructions to his sons not to have 'carnal copulation' with their wives. Cham thought that by being the first to produce a child, he would be able to 'disinherit the off-spring of his other two brethren'. Cham's disobedience thus showed 'contempt for Almighty God, and disobedience of parents'; God punished him by decreeing that his son Chus and all his posterity after him 'should be so black and loathsome, that it might remain a spectacle of disobedience to all the world. And of this black and cursed Chus came all these black Moores which are in Africa."[15] In medieval texts, Ham's story had been used to explain the servitude of European serfs.[16] Best inflects this class bias into a warning against greed about property and social mobility. He also suggests that Cham's sin (conventionally understood as seeing his father drunk and naked) is a *sexual transgression*. Moreover, in Best's story, it is Satan who prompts Cham and God who punishes him. Thus the account recirculates in a new form the already widespread associations of blackness with sexual excess and with the devil. Thus the story of Ham was used to denigrate and to interweave blackness, servitude, and sexual desire.

It has been suggested that Jewish commentaries on Noah's curse, or else Persian and Arab scholars, were responsible for introducing the element of blackness into the story of Ham.[17] Such suggestions need to be evaluated with great caution because they can deflect the blame for the enslavement of Africans onto the Jews, or else imply that 'Moors' were responsible for the very prejudices that were used against them. It is also important to remember that many versions of the Bible circulated in Europe, and that biblical stories were often misrepresented by authors who used them.

'Impossible things'

A correspondence between inner and outer being is complicated by the concept of religious conversion. Cesare Ripa's emblem book *Iconologia* depicts 'Religion' as a woman with a cross and fire standing against the motif of an elephant, reminding us how central the conversion of heathens and infidels was to European Christianity. Conversion implies that religious identity is not fixed or innate and can be acquired and shed. But this possibility generates two kinds of crisis. First, has the convert really converted? How can one tell if the outer show of conversion really matches up to an inner reality? Second, in the case of a dark-skinned person, conversion shatters the correspondence between inner faith and outer colour. Conversion thus creates a living contradiction, a person who is black outside and white inside.

Both these kinds of crises were heightened during the early modern period. All of Shakespeare's plays that explore the question of race repeatedly return to the question of conversion of one form or another: to its impossibility, or to the traumas it engenders or the social upheavals it can generate. Aaron the black Moor cannot be washed white, but Tamora the white Goth seems to be able to infiltrate Roman society for a while. Can Othello the Moor fully become 'of Venice', or Jessica the Jewess a real Christian? Is Shylock primarily a Jew or a merchant of Venice? Will association with Cleopatra turn Antony into an effeminate Egyptian? Can Caliban be civilized, or will he always retain something of his 'vile race'? Except in the case of Shylock and Jessica, religious conversion is not explicitly discussed in these plays. However, I suggest that the anxieties about identity that they manifest all have to do with the relationship between the inner and outer self. This relationship is at the heart of the question of religious conversion, as well as of emergent ideas about race in this period. In this section, we will look at the inner/outer debate as it is provoked by blackness.

There was a long tradition of speculating about the depth of skin colour. In the eleventh of Aesop's *Fables*, a man buys an 'Aethopian slave' and attempts to wash him white, thinking that the dark colour indicates bodily filth. In the Bible, black skin is used as a metaphor for an unchangeable essence:

Can the black Moor change his skin or the leopard his spots? *then* may ye also do good, that are accustomed to do evil.
Therefore will I scatter thee, as the stubble that is taken away with the South wind. (Jeremiah 13: 23)

Significantly, these words, which I have quoted from the 1560 edition of the Geneva Bible, are addressed to Jews. Throughout the early modern period, Jewish 'resistance' to Christianity is often compared to the permanence of black skin, as is made clear from the title of a seventeenth-century pamphlet, *The Blessed Jew of Marocco or a Black-moor made white*.[18]

Significantly, too, the earlier Bishop's Bible uses the words 'man of Ind' instead of 'black Moor'.[19] Thomas Palmer's *Two Hundred Poosees* (1565), England's earliest known emblem book, depicts, under the title 'Impossible things', two white men washing a black man (Fig. 4). The picture is accompanied by the following words:

4. A 'Man of Ind' from Thomas Palmer's emblem book *Two Hundred Poosees*.

> Why washhest thou the man of Ind?
>
> .   .   .   .   .
>
> Indurate heart of heretics
> Much blacker than the mole;
> With word or writ who seeks to purge
> Stark dead he blows the coal.[20]

Again, it is the stubborn 'heart of heretics' that is described as black and impossible to wash clean. Later, Geffrey Whitney's *A Choice of Emblemes* (1586), reproduced a similar picture with the title 'AEthiopem Lavare', and advised that it was useless to battle against the power of Nature and whiten the 'blackamore'.[21] So again we see a shift from 'man of Ind' to 'blackamore', which was also paralleled in stories about Ham's descendants who were located first in Asia and then in Africa. In all these books, blackness is evoked to make a point about the impossibility of religious conversions, but such impossibility in turn fixes black skin as indelible.

Renaissance dramas repeatedly play with this idea. In *Titus Andronicus*, Aaron turns it around to claim a superior position for blackness:

> Coal-black is better than another hue
> In that it scorns to bear another hue;
> For all the water in the ocean
> Can never turn the swan's black legs to white
>
> (4.2.98–101)

Because blackness is literally not washable, it needs to be compensated for by some other quality. In Webster's play *The White Devil*, a black serving girl called Zanche hopes that her dowry will allow a prospective white husband to overlook her black skin: 'make that sunburnt proverb false | And wash the Ethiope white' (5.2.248–9). Othello, the valiant general, mistakenly thinks that his record of bravery, the 'service' he has done the Venetian state has already had similar effect. Thus he relies on a radical *break* between his outer and inner self; as the Duke tells Brabanzio:

> If virtue no delighted beauty lack,
> Your son-in-law is far more fair than black.
>
> (1.3.289–90)

Othello thus problematizes the received equation of blackness with moral depravity, an equation that was being consolidated in Shakespeare's time by newer ideologies of race.

Conversion, Blackness, and Female Sexuality

In Shakespeare's *Love's Labour's Lost*, Biron invokes the vassalage of a 'rude and savage man of Ind' to describe his devotion to Rosaline. The lady herself, says, the king, is 'black as ebony' and therefore not worthy of such devotion; Biron counters by claiming that she is so beautiful that she is 'born to make black fair' (4.3.220, 245, 259). Biron's defence of his black beauty takes the form of an attack on women's face painting: other women paint themselves fair and therefore attract viewers with a 'false aspect' whereas his dark lady 'mourns that painting and usurping hair' (eschews make-up and false hair). So whereas other women 'dare not come in rain | For fear their colours should be washed away' (4.3.268–9) Biron's dark mistress is actually 'fair' by virtue of not wearing make-up.[22] This defence of black beauties rests upon an attack, fairly widespread at that time, upon the falsity of women who paint themselves. (Some of Shakespeare's Sonnets work along similar lines, and Sonnet 127 celebrates a 'black' mistress, lamenting women's tendency to 'put on nature's power | Fairing the foul with art's false borrowed face'.) The king responds by reiterating stereotypical abuse of blackness, and of black women in particular:

> Black is the badge of hell,
> The hue of dungeons and the style of night
>
> .   .   .   .   .
>
> No devil will fright thee so much as she.
>
> (4.3.250–1, 273)

Such debates about blackness reveal a deep ambivalence and unease about female beauty and sexuality. The image of woman as a white devil, harped on by moralists and preachers, suggested that a beguiling and beautiful exterior often concealed an evil interior. The criticism of face-painting also invoked a fear of the foreign, because cosmetics were supposed to be luxurious foreign imports and hence symbolic of the decadence of other cultures.

Black women were symbolically fêted at medieval courts—for instance, James IV of Scotland installed a black woman as the Queen of Beauty and himself appeared as a 'wild knight' who defended her. The lady's full lips, shining skin, and rich dress were described by the poet William Dunbar: the winner of the tournament was to be rewarded by the black lady's kiss while losers 'shall come behind and kiss her hips'.[23] Louise Olga Fradenburg astutely suggests that such black women worked as powerful emblems of royal power.[24] In feudal societies, she points out, women were routinely exchanged between various royal households, and therefore foreign queens were common at feudal courts. Common but disturbing, because there was a fear that if not properly assimilated, foreign queens would threaten the purity and integrity of the household and kingdom into which they had moved. Thus the ability of women to convert and adapt to new homes was essential for cultural and political stability, even as their supposed propensity for change-ability and duplicity aroused deep anxieties. By being able to master a foreign queen, the king displays his power over all his land and his subjects. The black lady of the tournament symbolizes both the danger of alien femininity, and its ultimate containment by the king.

By a similar logic, the praise of black beauty in Renaissance literature and art serves to emphasize the power of the artist, or the lover. Precisely because blackness was so powerfully equated with ugliness and fairness with beauty, to 'prove' through powerful poetic language that a black lady was fair is, in literary terms, to achieve the impossible and to wash the Ethiope white. Moreover, the conventional meanings of 'fair' and 'dark' are reinforced precisely by being momentarily displaced: the black beauty is more 'fair' than the fair woman who is actually 'dark' because false. The motif of a 'black but beautiful' woman and her containment by white masculinity is also central to religious writings, as can be seen from the 'Song of Songs', which is also known as the 'Song of Solomon' because it was erroneously attributed to that king of Israel. In this haunting love poem (originally a secular poem probably written in the third century BC and later assimilated into the Old as well as the New Testament), the central female figure declares:

I am dark, daughters of Jerusalem,
and I am beautiful!
Dark as the tents of Kedar, lavish
as Solomon's tapestries.[25]

Although (or perhaps because) the frank sexuality and passion of the
Song seems to be oddly placed in a religious book, medieval as well as
Renaissance commentaries on the Song interpreted it as an allegory
of spiritual, rather than erotic passion. They also changed the 'and'
between 'dark' and 'beautiful' to a 'but', positing a contradiction
between blackness and beauty so that black exterior of the woman
does not explain but clashes with her beauty. The blackness of the
woman was interpreted as representing the earthly suffering or the
sins of the believer, who was whitened through union with God and
by the power of repentance. Thus the black Bride of the Song of
Songs became a symbol for the tensions between earthly suffering and
spiritual redemption, with her fair male lover standing in for the
Church, or Christ himself. As we can see, such a reading easily maps
onto the figure of the dark-skinned convert, black outside but spir-
itually whitened by the power of Christ.

However, the spiritual interpretations of the Song were not innocent of social implications. Instead, their readings of blackness and
sexuality were overlaid with contemporary assumptions about geographic and ethnic difference, as Thomas Hahn demonstrates by
discussing an extraordinary passage from the letters of the medieval
divine Peter Abelard. Abelard's lover Heloise (like many others)
interpreted the Bride as 'an Ethiopian (such as the one Moses took
as a wife)'; Abelard replies:

The Ethiopian woman is black in the outer part of her flesh and as regards
exterior appearance looks less lovely than other women; yet she is not unlike
them within, but in several respects she is whiter and lovelier, in her bones,
for instance, or her teeth ... And so she is black without but lovely within; for
she is blackened outside in the flesh because in this life she suffers bodily
affliction ... Indeed the disfigurement of her blackness makes her choose
what is hidden rather than open, what is secret and not known to all, and
any such wife desires private, not public delights with her husband, and
would rather be known in bed than seen at table. Moreover it often happens
that the flesh of black women is all the softer to touch though it is less

attractive to look at, and for this reason the pleasure they give is greater and more suitable for private than for public enjoyment, and their husbands take them into a bedroom to enjoy them rather than parade them before the world.[26]

Here, Abelard's reading of the Bride as the suffering human body redeemed by Christ works by making the body of the black Ethiopian woman a symbol of sexual desire. The black female body is seen as both repulsive and desirable, to be enjoyed in secret even within marriage; the analogy implies that both blackness and sexuality are a guilty pleasure inviting duplicity, a private enjoyment that cannot be acknowledged in public. Travelogues and other writings echoed this idea—for example Peter Heylyn's *Microcosmus* suggested that the women of Barbary were 'beautiful in blackness, having delicate soft skins'.[27]

We can appreciate why commentaries on the Song often collapsed the figure of the Shulamite into that of the biblical Queen of Sheba, also referred to as the 'Queen of the South' and identified as the ruler of Saba or Ethiopia.[28] Sheba tested Solomon with 'hard questions', and when she was satisfied about his enormous wisdom, she gave the king 'a hundred and twenty talents of gold, and a very great quantity of spices, and precious stones; never again came such an abundance of spices as these which the queen gave to King Solomon'. The Bible also mentions that 'King Solomon gave unto Sheba all that she desired', a desire which was widely interpreted in sexual terms. This story, with its theme of sexual and economic exchange between a black queen and a lighter-skinned king was painted and retold all over Europe during the early modern period. Sheba was often depicted as black-skinned, and also read as a symbol of female lust and seductiveness. In Christian, Islamic as well as Jewish religious and folk traditions, the story became emblematic of the victory of faith over unbelief (Sheba was an unbeliever before being converted by Solomon) and of the patriarchal control of female sexuality.

Not surprisingly, these biblical motifs and tales acquired a special urgency as colonial contact began to proliferate. In ways that following chapters will discuss, Shakespeare's plays exploit this potential, revisiting and rewriting such scenarios. But in his plays, foreign queens and black men are not always submissive, and nor can they be whitened simply by converting to Christianity. In the Sonnets too, the black mistress is not just reassuringly 'natural' but also agonizingly sexual and promiscuous: thus she resonates with the figure of the lascivious 'Ethiope' or foreign woman that circulated in travel tales and other discourses of the period.

Artifice and Nature

Anxieties about skin colour, religious identity, and female sexuality all overlap; they also all hinge on the relationship between inner and outer being, between what is fixed or natural, and what is artificial and changeable. The racial and geographic connotations of this relationship are strikingly evident in John Bulwer's *Anthropometamorphoses: Man Transformed or the Artificiall Changeling Historically Presented* (1653). Although published after Shakespeare had died, this book is useful in understanding contemporary attitudes to race and sexuality because it assembles the opinions of a range of writers from Herodotus and Pliny to more contemporary medical and travel writings. In many of these writings, cultural and religious differences are understood to be manifested through physical or bodily characteristics, but Bulwer's text goes so far as to argue that cultural difference has the power to produce biological difference.

Bulwer suggests that English women have learnt face painting and other 'cosmetical conceits from Barbarous nations' (261) and that, in altering their bodies in a variety of ways, English people are widely imitating various foreign cultures. It argues that monsters are not found in nature but are artificially and culturally 'produced' all over the world by practices such as face and body painting, piercing, tattooing, circumcision, and various techniques of artificial elongation, compression, and moulding of body parts. However, once the body is altered by these cultural practices, Nature retaliates by reproducing the effect of these practices and bringing forth monsters at birth. Human symmetry, 'being casually, or purposely perverted, hath vigorously descended to their posterities, and that in durable deformities. This was the beginning of *Macrocephali*, or people with long heads. Thus have *Chineses* little feet, most *Negroes* great lips, and flat-Noses' (468). This is also how Bulwer explains stories of men with no heads, a staple feature of travel stories from classical times till the Renaissance.

Bulwer's explanation of colour difference is analogous: certain peoples find blackness beautiful, he says, and an 'Apish desire to change the complexion of their bodies' motivates them to colour themselves black:

And so from this artifice the Moors might possibly become Negroes...And this complexion, first by art acquired, might be evidently maintained by generation, and by the tincture of the skin, as a spermatical part traduced from father to son. For thus perhaps this which at the beginning of this complexion was an artificial device, and thus induced by imagination, having once impregnated the seed, found afterwards concurrent productions, which were continued by climes, whose constitution advantaged the artificial into a natural impression. (469)

This extraordinary passage makes explicit the difference between 'Moors' and 'Negroes', arguing that cultural work or 'the imagination' has the power to alter the body genetically. Of course early modern medicine did not work with the concept of genes as such but the phrase 'spermatical part traduced from father to son' expresses a hereditary element. The idea that our thoughts, or imaginations, can bring about bodily change was not unique to Bulwer: women were widely supposed to produce children who were imprints of either their secret desires or of images that they had seen during the sexual act. The implication was that not just sexual acts, but also sexual desires, need to be policed in order to preserve genealogical purity. Bulwer specifically connects this idea to the origin of blackness.

Bulwer describes most of these practices as originating in Africa, Asia, or America: thus it is the racial others of Europe who initiate the sin of artifice, of 'taking God's pencil in their own hands' and being punished by a permanent deformation.[29] The whole book is written as a warning to English people about the dangers of imitating such foreign practices. In a final section called 'The Pedigree of the English Gallant', Bulwer juxtaposes foreign bodies with English ones, graphically illustrating his argument that English people were widely imitating barbaric peoples and were in danger of mutating into the latter (Fig. 5). Although Bulwer accuses men as well as women of painting and imitating foreign cosmetic practices, he singles

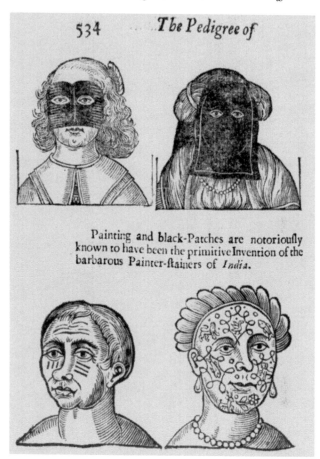

5 (*a–b*). English fashions imitate the face painting and other artifices of foreign people (see also p. 66). John Bulwer, *Anthropometamorphoses*.

out women (European as well as non-European) for initiating such artifice. He suggests that the men of the 'race' of Ham have enormous penises because midwives who deliver them do not 'close knit' their 'navel-strings'. Thus those physical features that were important to the emerging discourse of race, such as skin colour and sexual organs, are explained as originating in artifice, of which women are

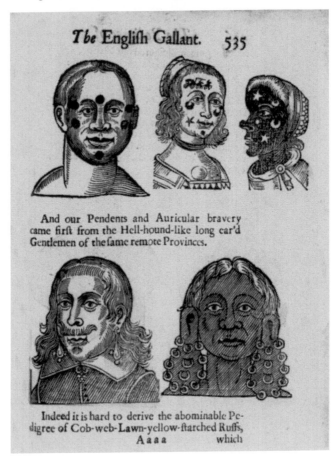

The Englifh Gallant.   535

And our Pendents and Auricular bravery
came firft from the Hell-hound-like long ear'd
Gentlemen of the fame remote Provinces.

Indeed it is hard to derive the abominable Pedigree of Cob-web-Lawn-yellow-ftarched Ruffs,
     A a a a   which

(*b*)

the supreme practitioners: 'If this supposition be true', Bulwer laments,
'we are all at the mercy of the Midwives for our sufficiency' (401).

Montaigne's famous essay 'Of Cannibals' had taken an opposite
position from Bulwer's, arguing that it is non-Europeans who live
closer to Nature, and Europeans whose civilization consists of
artifice. The Brazilians, whom Europeans call cannibals and barbaric
are 'wild, just as we call wild the fruits that Nature has produced by

herself and in her normal course; whereas really it is those that we have changed artificially and led astray from the common order that we should call wild'.[30] Over time, Montaigne's essay fed into the idea of the noble and childlike savage, who retains a primordial innocence. Shakespeare invokes it twice: in old Gonzalo's ruminations upon the island in *The Tempest*, and in Polixenes and Perdita's exchange about grafting in *The Winter's Tale*.

Conversions and the New Racism

The last chapter argued that the fact that the Renaissance had not yet fully acquired the notion of biologically fixed 'races' is not necessarily a sign of its liberalism or tolerance, but only a reflection of contemporary beliefs about the human body. Critics have often interpreted religion as cultural, and the physical body as racial, but I have been suggesting that this equation is not helpful in tracing changing ideas about race. The indelibility of blackness, we have seen, is often expressed in the context of the difficulty of a change of faith. It is not surprising that beliefs about physical and cultural difference were brought to a crisis by the phenomenon of religious conversion.

Conversion was a volatile and pressing concern all over early modern Europe, both in relation to outsiders and vis-à-vis domestic populations. Authorities constantly outlawed certain faiths or sects, whose followers had to convert or leave. The most spectacular examples are the expulsions of Jews and Moors, but schisms within Christianity also resulted in persecutions and conversions. After Jews were officially expelled from England in 1290, about 2,000 to 2,500 were deported and others had to live as converts.[31] Spain also expelled Jews in 1492, as did Portugal shortly afterwards, and in all these situations only converts to Christianity, derogatorily called 'Marranos' (or swine) could stay on. From that year on, forcible conversions of the Moors also began all over Spain, and from 1609, over a million converts (called 'Moriscoes') were expelled. In England too, which swung between Protestant and Catholic regimes, a change of faith was often necessary for survival. Thus, in James Shapiro's words, religious faith was like 'a role one could assume or discard if one had sufficient improvisational skill' (17). But it was a disguise that did not always work, and those in power suspected converts of secretly adhering to their old faith. In Spain, converted Moors were suspected of mocking Christianity through their music and dance, which were forbidden, as was writing in Arabic. Even the fertility of Morisco women was seen by the Christian authorities as an indication that the converts would soon outnumber the Old Christians.[32] Similarly, even if they occupied important public posts and professions, many converted Jews were suspected of secretly nurturing Judaism.

In 1480, the Inquisition, which met at Seville, introduced the idea that religious faith was manifested in 'purity of blood' (*limpieza de sangre*). Those among the Spanish nobility who had fought to keep out Moorish invaders in the eighth century were regarded as the purest, those who had nurtured Moors or Jews at any point were seen as less pure, and the least pure were converted Jews and Moors. The converts could hardly prove their purity of blood and many fled the country. Many commentators regard these blood laws as the crucial turning point in the history of race. [33] Religious faith was now seen as an inner essence that transmitted itself over generations, as is made clear in this passage from a Spanish biography of Charles V:

Who can deny that in the descendants of the Jews there persists and endures the evil inclination of their ancient ingratitude and lack of understanding, just as in Negroes [there persists] the inseparability of their blackness? For if the latter should unite themselves a thousand times with white women, the children are born with the dark colour of the father. Similarly, it is not enough for a Jew to be three parts aristocratic or Old Christian for one family-line alone defiles and corrupts him.[34]

The important point about this passage is that some internal essence is seen to be responsible for the Jews' 'ingratitude' as well as the Negroes' blackness, an essence that survives even when mixed with white Christian blood.

At the most obvious level, Jews and 'Negroes' pose *opposite* kinds of problems. Because most European Muslims and Jews were not darker than Christians, conversions between these religions could be both easily imagined and considered slippery: how could a Spanish Moor (or indeed an English Jew) be detected after conversion? On the other hand, the black Moor or 'Negro' always stood out, and in this case the problem is heightened not by a false conversion but a real one. In neither case is a correspondence between outer appearance and inner being suggested, but by comparing the persistence of Jewish 'ingratitude' with black skin colour, one 'inner' quality with another 'outer' one, the passage renders both congenital. Again, women were at the centre of such discourses, and it was feared that the milk of Jewish wet-nurses, 'being of infected persons' would 'engender perverse inclinations' in any Old Christian children they suckled.[35] Exactly the same language is used in a very different context by Spenser's *View of the State of Ireland* which describes English people 'fostering and marrying with the Irish' as 'the two most dangerous infections' and expresses the fear of Irishness passing into English children's bodies through the milk of Irish mothers and wet-nurses.[36]

The Spanish 'blood laws' interpreted differences of faith as signs of different interior essences; faith is therefore not a matter of choice. Of course this idea was not suddenly born in early modern Spain—as we saw, the comparison of Jewish faith to black skin is evident in English writings. Also, the idea of an irreducible Jewish essence can be traced back to earlier times, as is illustrated by the story of Anaclet II, the 'Jewish Pope'. During the Schism in the twelfth century, he was one of the rival popes and even though his family had converted to Christianity a century earlier, his opponents denounced him for his Jewish ancestry. The attacks focused on his descent from 'the people who had killed Christ', claimed that he had risen to his position because of his family's moneylending activities, and suggested that he had sex with 'nuns, married women, and even with his own sister, copulating at random as though he were a dog'.[37] Thus, a century after his family converted, a Jewish essence, supposedly manifest in religious, economic, and sexual habits, was seen to persist in Anaclet. However, in early modern Spain, the question of conversions was posed on an enormous scale, and with respect not just to Moors and Jews within the country, but to the inhabitants of Spanish colonies abroad. The blood laws had contradicted the Christian declaration that all humans are descended from the same protoplasm. As colonialism advanced, these contradictions deepened as increasing numbers of non-Europeans were simultaneously invited to convert to Christianity and described as biologically different from Europeans.

In England too, questions of conversion were culturally central, as citizens had to turn, 'just like the Weathercock, with the breath of every Prince', as one writer put it, between various shades of Catholicism and Protestantism.[38] England was also flooded with stories of Christians who were captured by Turkish armies or North African pirates and forced to convert to Islam, or 'turn Turk'. The preacher Henry Byam accused such men of oscillating between Christianity and Islam according to their convenience: 'many hundreds are Musselmans in Turkey, and Christians at home; doffing their religion, as they do their clothes, and keeping a conscience for every harbor where they shall put in.'[39] In England too, religion was sometimes discussed in quasi-biological terms: Byam's co-preacher Edward Kellet, for example, railed against 'these Christian-Jews or Jewish Christians [who] would join Moses and Christ, forgetting the substance of the precepts given unto them . . . *Thou shalt not let thy cattle gender with diverse kind, thou shalt not sow thy field with a mingled seed.*'[40]

Fears that outward appearances might not match inner beliefs were exacerbated by the fact that 'Jew', 'Moor', or 'Christian' were never simply religious categories, but always complicated by nationality, ethnicity, and often colour. Phrases such as 'A Christian-Jew' or 'a Turk, but a Cornish man born' attested to the fact that religion and location were understood as affiliations which conversions could not entirely erase.[41] Everywhere, overseas contact (through colonialism, trade, or the slave trade) amplified the crisis about conversion and racial identity.

Moorish Difference

Historically, Protestant England's enmity with Catholic Spain complicated its attitude to Moors. Elizabeth I was engaged in an effort to consolidate English trading ties with Morocco, especially in arms. Some critics suggest that for this reason the English could not have held a purely negative view of Moors. Official as well as popular opinion occasionally suggested that there was special affinity between Protestants and Muslims who were both enemies of 'Idolators'. The prosperous merchant Edmund Hogan who was involved in the arms trade with Morocco claimed that the Moroccan Emperor 'Abd-el-Malik, 'beareth a greater affection to our Nation than to others because of our religion, which forbiddeth worship of Idols, and the

Moores called him the Christian King'.[42] The Turks too were potential trading partners for the English, and therefore Queen Elizabeth
herself claimed that both she and the Great Turk were enemies to
idolaters, a sentiment that was often reciprocated by the Turks themselves.

But it would be misleading to select expressions of anti-Catholic
solidarity between the English and the Islamic powers with whom
they wanted to trade in order to present an uncomplicated picture of
affinity between the English and 'Moors'. Whatever attractions the
new mercantile networks held for the English were complicated by a
long history of animosity. State policies and alliances, as well as non-
official attitudes among Protestants constantly fluctuated—Martin
Luther at first suggested that Turks were the scourge of God against
Catholic sins, but when the Sultan's army approached Vienna he
advocated war against them. Of course, the trading potential of
Turks and Moroccans no doubt conferred upon them a kind of
glamour and stature. In August 1600, about a year before *Othello* was
written, London welcomed an embassy from the court of the Moroccan Emperor 'Abd-el-Malik which stayed in the city for nearly six
months.[43] A contemporary portrait depicts an aristocratic Moor, a
well-dressed and somewhat menacing figure (Fig. 6). The embassy,
and the portrait, certainly affirm that English could not have thought
of all 'Moors' as black slaves, but they do not prove that they were
viewed simply as glamorous allies. A court official's letter reported that
English merchants and mariners had refused 'to carry them into
Turkey, because they think it a matter odious and scandalous to the
world to be friendly or familiar with Infidels . . .'.[44]

This letter reminds us that all responses to Muslims could not be
entirely moulded by official policy. A deep-seated hostility to Islam
had been shaped by the long legacy of the Crusades, which in turn
was filtered through legends of Muslim invasions and of Moorish
misdeeds in Spain, and these were compounded by renewed fear of
Ottoman expansion. Distinctions between Saracens, Turks, and Moroccans (all of whom could be referred to as 'Moors') were often not
clear in English writings. In popular literature, Muslims were not
always depicted as potential allies of the Protestants. Just as often, an
unholy connection between Muslims and Roman Catholics was
suggested, as in this poem by John Phillips:

6. Portrait of the Moroccan ambassador to the court of Elizabeth I.

> If Mahomet, that prophet false,
> Eternity do gain,
> Then shall the Pope, and you his saints,
> In heaven be sure to reign.[45]

Like Judaism, Islam was especially threatening to Christians because it often contested the same scriptural lineage, and because it had coexisted with Christianity in the very heart of Europe.

By the sixteenth century, Islam was widely viewed as a 'uncleane Bird' that had been bred in Arabia, a 'poison' and a 'pestilence' that had 'infected' a large part of Asia, as well as Africa, and would overrun Europe if it was not checked.[46] *The Notable History of Saracens* (1578) wanted to trace the success of 'this pestilent Generation' in order to warn readers of that Christian unity was necessary to face the renewed threat they posed:

They were (indeed) at first very far off from our clime and region, and therefore the less to be feared, but now they are even at our doors and ready to come into our houses, if our penitent hearts do not the sooner procure at the merciful hands of God, an untie peace and concord among the princes, potentates and people of that little portion of Christendom yet left, which through division, discord and civil dissention hath from time to time enticed and brought this Babylonian Nabugadnezar and Turkish Pharao so near under our noses. (Epistle Dedicatory)

In plays such as Fletcher's *The Island Princess* and Massinger's *The Renegado*, the fear of a Moorish enemy serves to unite various squabbling European factions and make them realize that a much deeper divide exists between all Christians on the one hand and Moors or heathens on the other.

Nabil Matar has suggested that it was only English theological and literary texts that betrayed a hostility to Muslims: 'it was the stereotype developed in literature that played the greatest role in shaping anti-Muslim national consciousness.'[47] The court letter, histories, and travelogues quoted above (and in the rest of this book) complicate this generalization, but even if we concur with Matar's argument that literary texts registered the greatest anxiety about Muslims, it is hard to agree with his claim that 'in their discourse about Muslims, Britons produced a representation that did not belong to the actual encounter with the Muslims' but was 'borrowed . . . from their encounter with American Indians' (15). Any understanding of the 'actual encounter' cannot ignore the historical-cultural lens through which each party views the other. Literary texts are crucial indices of cultural complexities, rather than fictions superimposed upon them. Secondly, our analysis of racial ideologies and stereotyping has to go beyond identifying 'positive' or 'negative' images and taking these at face value. English writings acknowledge Turkish military superiority, civic organization, and patriarchal control. They envy and even want to emulate these attributes, but at the same time, they see these as evidence of an alien and threatening culture. Evidence of Muslim power only feeds into the construction of Muslim alterity in this period.

This is evident even in a play such as George Peele's *The Battle of Alcazar* (1589), which splits Moors into black and white, treacherous and upright. This play rewrites the historical battle of Alcazar (1578) between Sebastian, king of Portugal, and 'Abd-el-Malik, emperor of Morocco, known in England as Abdelmelec. Contemporary reports tried to explain the Christian defeat in this battle by blaming Sebastian's reliance on 'Abd-el-Malik's rebellious nephew. Peele's play portrays Abdelmelec as an honourable and fair Moor of impeccable Islamic lineage, while Muly Hamet, his nephew, is a Negro-Moor', 'Black in his look, and bloody in his deeds . . . Accompanied, as now you may behold | With devils coated in the shapes of men'.[48] These divisions are common in contemporary travelogues and plays. In order to maintain them, however, Peele's play has to downplay the fact that Sebastian's is a 'holy Christian war' to 'plant the Christian faith' and 'religious truth in Africa' (2.492). Abdelmelec becomes less a religious adversary and more a noble king fighting against a usurper. By the end, the black Muly absorbs Christian antipathy to Islam as well as to blackness. The Portuguese King Sebastian attributes to him the negative traits widely associated with Muslims:

> False-hearted Mahomet, now to my cost
> I see thy treachery, warn'd to beware
> A face so full of fraud and villainy.

$$(4.284\text{--}6)$$

It is to be noted that he calls Muly 'Mahomet', the name of the Prophet, who was repeatedly represented as a trickster. The punishment for Muly makes his black skin into a spectacle of warning—he is to be skinned and stuffed with straw 'to deter and fear the lookers-on | From any such foul fact or bad attempt' (4.468–9). Shakespeare's *Titus Andronicus* ends on a similar note, and along with *Othello*, it allows us to understand the dynamics of the separation as well as the tense interplay between religion and skin colour.

Wilderness and Civilization
in Titus Andronicus

Ravenous Tigers

In their account of staging *Titus Andronicus* (1594) in apartheid-scarred South Africa, Antony Sher and Gregory Doran describe how black audiences identified so powerfully with Aaron, the black villain of the play, that they 'cheer him right the way through the plot to rape Lavinia', backing off only when he hacks off Titus' hand. When Aaron defies Tamora's order to kill their black child, saying 'Tell the empress from me, I am of age | To keep mine own, excuse it how she can' (4.2.103–4), the entire house erupted:

'Yebo!' the audience shriek out, 'Yebo!' yelling their approval and solidarity. A memorable show.

Afterwards standing in the bar, one of them comes up to us, 'I didn't understand it all here', he says, pointing to his head. Then he bangs his chest, 'But I understood it here'.[1]

It is not surprising that black South Africans who had long been struggling to affirm that they were of age and competence to govern themselves, 'to keep their own', would forge emotional bonds with Aaron. In other situations, it is harder to interpret Aaron as an *exposure* of the demonization of blackness. Directors have sometimes edited the play severely in order to elevate Aaron 'into a noble and lofty character', as happened when the famous Ira Aldridge played the role in 1857.[2]

Because Aaron is a textbook illustration for early modern stereo-types of blackness, his skin colour has never been disputed in the same way that Othello's has. But it is harder to agree on what these stereotypes meant to Renaissance audiences. In an important essay, G. K. Hunter suggested that 'The Moor, like the Jew (but with less obvious justification) is seen primarily in religious terms'.[3] Hunter is correct that blackness was seen as a sign of Islamic depravity, or a moral flaw, but he counterposes 'religion' to 'race', an 'old framework of assumptions about Jews, Turks and Moors' to 'true facts about these remote races' (53). More recently, John Gillies traces the influence of Greek and Roman myths of 'barbarism' and 'exoticism' upon all of Shakespeare's pictures of 'others'. He also points out that during the Renaissance, the classics were interpreted through the Bible; therefore, for Renaissance writers and audiences, classical ideas about barbarians would be filtered through religious notions of depravity.[4] But, in Gillies's view, an emphasis on the force of an 'ancient poetic geographic economy of difference' is valuable in indicating how the 'construction of otherness in Shakespeare ... is *completely independent* of the anachronistic terminology of "race", "colour" and "prejudice"' (25; emphasis added). Like Hunter, Gillies identifies an important frame of reference but then isolates it from newer dynamics of inter-cultural contact. Constructions of 'barbarism' and 'blackness' even in the medieval period, let alone in an early modern one, were shaped by contemporary religious, geopolitical, and cultural tensions. Such tensions were most often expressed through older vocabularies, it is true, and by resurrecting what appear to be outmoded stereotypes. But I believe we must combine literary and textual histories with political and cultural ones, as Kim Hall does in her analysis of blackness in early modern culture, if we are to make any sense of figures such as Aaron. As this chapter will show, older stereotypes about barbarism, black sexuality, and evil evoked by Aaron mediate newer anxieties about nation, religion, race, and femininity.

Shakespeare's earliest tragedy is set in the fourth century AD, when the Roman Empire was waning, and it opens with military violence undertaken in the name of patriotism. At the culmination of Rome's 'weary wars against the barbarous Goths' (1.1.28), the general Titus Andronicus returns home, having 'brought to yoke' the enemies of Rome, and leading in his prisoners who include Tamora, queen of the Goths and her three sons. He himself has lost all but four of his twenty-five sons, and one of them, Lucius, now demands a Goth prisoner 'to sacrifice his flesh' in the memory of his dead brothers. Titus, deaf to Tamora's maternal pleas, gives Lucius her eldest son Alarbus 'T'appease their groaning shadows that are gone'. Lucius graphically anticipates the ritual: 'Let's hew his limbs till they be clean consumed,' he says, and also relishes describing the deed afterwards. This bloody murder, performed in the name of Roman tradition and religion, inaugurates a spiral of increasing violence, each deed responding to, and exceeding the previous one. Tamora and her sons avenge Alarbus' death by raping and mutilating Titus' daughter Lavinia, killing his son-in-law Bassianus, and implicating Titus' sons Martius and Quintus in Bassianus' murder. In return, Titus executes an elaborate revenge in which he kills Tamora's sons Chiron and Demetrius, and bakes them in a pie which he serves to Tamora before killing her. He himself is stabbed by Tamora's husband, the Roman emperor Saturninus, who in turn is killed by Titus' son Lucius. This chain of revenge is complicated by other acts of violence, notably Titus' murder of his own son Mutius and daughter Lavinia, the former because he has helped Bassianus elope with Lavinia against Titus' wishes, and the latter because she has been ravished and mutilated by Tamora's sons. Thus both the nation and the family require violence against outsiders but also against disobedient insiders.

Although almost every character participates in this gory violence, at the end of the play two people are singled out as pariahs who must be cast out so that Rome can be restored to civility and health. One of them, Tamora, is already dead, but even so, Lucius orders that her body must be thrown out of the city walls to 'beasts and birds of prey'. The other, Aaron, her black servant and lover, is called 'the chief architect and plotter of these woes' and 'breeder of these dire events' (5.3.120, 177); Lucius commands:

> Set him breast-deep in earth and famish him.
> There let him stand, and rave, and cry for food.
> If anyone relieves or pities him,
> For the offence he dies.

(5.3.178–81)

If imperial Rome has degenerated into a 'wilderness of tigers' where civility and justice have been abandoned, the two outsiders, Aaron and Tamora, each of whom is called a 'ravenous tiger', are held responsible. Like Iago, Aaron has directed some of the violent events in the play, suggesting to Chiron and Demetrius that they not only rape Lavinia, but cut off her tongue as well as her arms. This plan is based on, but also exceeds, Ovid's story of Philomel, who was raped by her brother-in-law King Tereus. Although Philomel's tongue was cut off, she was able to reveal the identity of her rapist by weaving a tapestry. Aaron, a barbarian who has no civility in him, not only knows these stories central to Roman culture, but is able to use and 'improve' upon them, confirming his status as a 'devil' who is dangerous because he possesses intimate knowledge of the human world. He is, as Marcus says, 'a craftier Tereus' (2.4.41) who also invents new tales, telling Titus that Saturninus will spare his two sons if he is given a hand belonging to Titus, his brother, or son.

But despite all this activity and ingenuity, Aaron is not really the 'chief architect' of the plot in the same sense as Iago, to whom he is often compared. Iago is, of course, the Shakespearian villain most often associated with 'motiveless malignity' (Samuel Taylor Coleridge's words for him). However, Iago can be regarded as 'motiveless' only if we ignore his racial and class envy of Othello, the black outsider who has risen to the top of Venetian society and who is now in a position to evade Iago's requests to him with 'bombast circumstance'. Can we understand Aaron's villainy in analogous terms, as an attempt to rise above his station as slave? Act 2 opens with an extraordinary soliloquy in which Aaron meditates upon Tamora's climb to 'Olympus's top', following her marriage to Saturninus:

> Then, Aaron, arm thy heart and fit thy thoughts
> To mount aloft with thy imperial mistress,
> And mount her pitch whom thou in triumph long
> Hast prisoner held fettered in amorous chains
>
> .   .   .   .   .
>
> I will be bright, and shine in pearl and gold
> To wait upon this new-made empress.
> To wait, said I?—to wanton with this queen,
> This goddess, this Semiramis, this nymph,
> This siren that will charm Rome's Saturnine
> And see his shipwreck...
>
> (2.1.12–15, 19–24)

Aaron's desire to 'mount aloft' with, and 'mount' his 'imperial mistress' reminds his audience that she is his mistress in both senses—his lover as well as his owner. Perhaps one way for Aaron to ensure her continuing dependence upon him is by taking charge of her revenge against the Romans. Her position as empress may bring him such benefits as pearl and gold clothes, but Aaron recognizes that her victory over the Romans may also bring real power for him. Thus, when Tamora invites him to make love with her, he tells her that 'though Venus govern your desires, | Saturn is dominator over mine', that 'Vengeance is in my heart, death in my hand' (2.3.30–1, 38). While in this particular scene Aaron departs from the stereotype of the lusty Moor, he only does so by confirming another, that of black malignity.

As Aaron becomes increasingly vocal and active, he repeatedly describes himself as a person whose blackness and villainy explain each other. For most characters in this play, but also, disturbingly, for Aaron himself, blackness is a moral quality. His exterior appearance indicates an inner propensity for evil—his 'woolly hair' is like an 'adder' uncurling 'To do some fatal execution' (2.3.34–6) and his inner being is reflected in his skin colour:

> Let fools do good, and fair men call for grace:
> Aaron will have his soul black like his face.
>
> (3.1.203–4)

Thus Aaron revels in the fact that he cannot be 'washed white': 'Coal-black is better than another hue | In that it scorns to bear another hue' (4.2.98–9). Whiteness is inferior to blackness because the latter will not register other colours, either through a blush, sunburn, or paint.

Aaron is a 'swart Cimmerian' whose body is not just dark but 'spotted, detested and abominable', and a foil to the 'white and spotless' robes which are sent to Titus when he is elected as Roman emperor; he is the 'barbarous Moor', a 'hellish dog', an 'incarnate devil', a 'wall-eyed slave' with a 'fiendish face', an 'accursed devil'. The violence underlying such invective is underscored in the scene where Titus reproaches Marcus for killing a 'poor harmless fly'. When Marcus explains 'it was a black ill-favoured fly, | Like to the Empress' Moor', Titus begs his pardon:

> For thou hast done a charitable deed.
> Give me thy knife. I will insult on him,
> Flattering myself as if it were the Moor.

(3.2.70–3)

Remarkably, other people's invectives against Aaron's blackness are not just corroborated, but amplified and extended, by his own self-assessments. He claims that there has not been a day in which he has not committed some crime,

> As kill a man, or else devise his death;
> Ravish a maid, or plot the way to do it;
> Accuse some innocent and forswear myself;
> Set deadly enmity between two friends;
> Make poor men's cattle break their necks;
> Set fire on barns and haystacks in the night,
> And bid the owners quench them with their tears.
> Oft I have digged up dead men from their graves
> And set them upright at their dear friends' door,
> Even when their sorrows almost was forgot,
> And on their skins, as on the bark of trees,
> Have with my knife carvèd in Roman letters
> 'Let not your sorrow die though I am dead.'
> But I have done a thousand dreadful things
> As willingly as one would kill a fly,
> And nothing grieves me heartily indeed
> But that I cannot do ten thousand more.

(5.1.128–44)

Whereas Titus worries about killing a harmless fly, Aaron thinks of human beings as flies, to be destroyed at will.

This lengthy catalogue is strikingly similar to the list of his crimes offered by Barabas the Jew in Marlowe's play *The Jew of Malta*. Aaron's name is of Jewish origin too, reminding us that overlapping stereotypes of Jews and Moors go back to the Crusades. Shylock in *The Merchant of Venice* is also called 'dog' and 'devil', and some Renaissance plays show the two as allies plotting the downfall of Christians. The analogy between Muslims and Jews was sometimes literalized with Jews being represented as black. But whereas Muslims and Jews were feared and hated for their adherence to a different faith, many black 'Moors', as we've seen, were increasingly viewed as godless, an image that Aaron relishes. Does Aaron's exultation in his own wickedness indicate his defiant attempt to control a hostile environment and to manipulate a society in whose eyes he can do no good anyway? While Aaron's attitude anticipates certain strategies of defiance among twentieth-century black political movements, such as their appropriation and inversion of terms such as 'bad,' or their endorsement of violence as a strategy of fighting back, his delight in crime is presented as haphazard, connected not to his race or class consciousness, but to his race and class themselves. Thus it only confirms the notion of the motiveless malignity of blacks.

Is Aaron just a stock figure of black villainy? Does Shakespeare simply reiterate an older stereotype, or does this play also bear the impress of newer developments? An equation between certain physical characteristics and inner qualities was part of medieval discourses about race, but as we saw, it was also crucial to the new, more biological, views of racial difference. Aaron's baseness is reinforced by the status as a slave. 'Race', as discussed earlier, was a term most often used to describe class status, and 'villain' was a word that originally referred to someone low-born. Aaron's servile status confirms the moral depravity of black people, whereas Othello's royal birth contradicts that idea. Earlier, we noted that in medieval times there were two distinct though overlapping ways of understanding blackness—one, in which it signified monstrousness, bestiality, and godlessness, the other in which it symbolized religious difference, especially Islam. The difference between these two is underlined in new ways in the early modern period. Muslims are still often pictured as physically as well as morally 'black', but the difference between them and the irreligious Moor is marked, and expressed, in terms of class, culture, and location. North African or Arab Moors, being Muslim, are allowed a cultural lineage, religious traditions, and occasionally a lighter skin colour. Sub-Saharan Africans are increasingly associated with a lack of religion and culture, and painted as low-born. While 'blackamoors' and men of 'Ind' are depicted as naked or shackled, Turks and other Muslims are pictured as elaborately clothed and turbaned. The difference between the two is not that the Muslim Moor is regarded as 'good' and the black Moor as 'bad', but rather that the latter stereotype develops in tandem with the fast emerging slave trade, whereas the former responds to other historical tensions.

Disassociating a people from their own lineage, religion, and culture facilitates their dehumanization; thus the older stereotype of the black bestiality takes on new and more specific geopolitical resonance in the early colonial world.

Aaron knows Rome well, but his only reference to a world outside the Roman or Gothic one is his mention of his 'countryman' Muliteus. Muly was the most common name given to Moors in the drama of the period, and in *Titus* we have no idea what country Aaron or Muliteus might have come from. Minus any religion or specific origins, Aaron exists solely in a white world, using its tales and myths to manufacture his own stories. For all his wickedness, Aaron only intervenes in and redirects a dynamic of rivalry and revenge between the Goths and the Romans whose logic has already been set in motion. Aaron's tale is powerful and spectacular, but unlike Iago's, in the larger scheme of things it is but a footnote to the text of Roman-Gothic rivalry, which sets the real agenda of the play. It is there that the overlap between civility and barbarism becomes most apparent, and allows us to see why we have a figure of black malignity in a play which is otherwise about the Gothic-Roman wars.

By definition empires need to expand, to annex territories and peoples outside themselves into their boundaries, and as they do so, to underline differences between themselves and those they conquer. Roman assertions of their own civility depend upon an opposition between themselves and the 'barbarous' Goths: 'Thou art a Roman,' Marcus tells his brother Titus, 'be not barbarous' (1.1.375). The oppositions between 'Goth' and 'Roman' are rapidly dismantled by the play—when Lucius demands Alarbus as a sacrificial victim, Tamora points out that her parental sentiments should be recognizable to Titus, who has lost so many children. In Shakespeare's plays, the idea of a humanity shared across religious or national boundaries is often evoked by those characters who are victims of, and yet subscribe to, ideologies of 'difference'. In *The Merchant of Venice*, for example, Shylock slyly uses it to defend his infamous bond. Tamora rightly tells Titus that her sons were only doing for their country what Titus' were for theirs:

> if to fight for king and commonweal
> Were piety in thine, it is in these.
>
> (1.1.114–15)

But for Titus to acknowledge these similarities would be for him to undermine the reason he has fought the Goths. He insists on the violent 'Roman rite' which only confirms the incivility of Rome: Tamora calls it 'irreligious piety' and Chiron comments that Scythia (a region north of the Black Sea considered to lie beyond the margins of civilization) was never 'half so barbarous' (1.1.130–1).

The revenges of Tamora and her clan on the one hand, and those of Titus and his on the other, continue to mirror each other. By the end, the opposition between barbarism and civility has been so rearranged that the Goths become crucial agents in the righting of the Roman order. But each side is also fractured—the schisms among Romans are evident in the opening act itself, and later there is a divide between the Goths and their erstwhile queen, who has already aligned herself with one Roman faction in order to revenge herself upon the other. Critics have debated whether or not there are two different sets of Goths in the play, with Tamora and her sons representing a 'barbaric' faction, and the ones who help Lucius at the end of the play a more humane one.[5] In Elizabethan England, the Goths were viewed as brutish and lawless, but also as ancestors of the English. On the other hand, the Romans were both conquerors of England and imperialists worthy of English emulation. Jonathan Bate suggests that the Goths were also equated with Germans, so that the play may be suggesting that Roman imperial decadence (represented by Saturninus and his court) needs to be countered by the 'plain outdoor virtue of the Teutonic tribes'.[6] The crucial point is that by the end of the play, the Goths and Romans unite in what one critic calls a '"Rainbow Coalition", similar to those multi-racial, multi-ethnic groups found in contemporary society, between Romans and Goths to purge Rome'.[7]

Are Goths and Romans indeed different races, and if so, how is their 'Rainbow Coalition' forged? Tamora attempts to cross the lines between the two groups; her marriage to Saturninus elevates the 'barbarous' queen to the position of empress of Rome. Her relationship with Saturninus is not viewed with the same horror as is her liaison with Aaron. Because of the status of the Goths as a 'barbarous' people subject to imperial Roman violence, critics sometimes suggest that she is not quite white (a move that is analogous to critics' whitening Othello because he abides by the rules of Venetian civility). Saturninus finds her attractive from the beginning, remarking that she is

> a goodly lady, trust me, of the hue
> That I would choose were I to choose anew.
>
> (1.1.261–2)

She is of the right 'hue', unlike Aaron the 'swart Cimmerian' who, by his sexual contact with her, makes her 'honour of his body's hue, | Spotted, detested and abominable' (2.3.72–4). As a white though foreign queen, her marriage to the Emperor Saturninus is not unthinkable in a feudal dynastic world in which both war and intermarriage between different groups and kingdoms were widespread. Even if she had not been royal, such an alliance would not have been scandalous because it would have preserved existing hierarchies of gender and rank, and because her whiteness would at least visually preserve racial purity. The marriage is considered inappropriate not on racial grounds but because it reveals Tamora's ability to manipulate her way to power. Thus her behaviour as an ambitious woman, and her association with Aaron define Tamora's status as alien, rather than any racial difference from the Romans. Of course, we should keep in mind that alien races were defined precisely through their departure from normative gender behaviour. But in the end, even the Goths are shocked by her affair with Aaron, which sets her apart from them, and helps advance the new Gothic-Roman alliance.

The scandal of Aaron's alliance with Tamora most drastically minimizes the distance between the Goths and the Romans, who, in spite of mutual distrust and enmity, consider themselves far more distant from Aaron the Moor than from each other. Except Tamora, who repeatedly calls him 'lovely', everyone in the play thinks of Aaron's colour as foul or ugly. Even the docile Lavinia insults Tamora for her 'experiments' with 'her raven-coloured love' (2.3.69, 83). Despite the fact that one of them can at least pretend to be 'incorporate in Rome', while the other can only be the object of Roman scorn and hatred, Tamora and Aaron are both called by similar names—'barbarous' (2.3.118, 78) and 'ravenous tiger' (5.3.5,194). One is literally raven coloured while the other is compared to a raven. If Aaron is 'inhuman', Tamora is a 'beastly creature' who is compared to a tiger, and a bear, who has 'no grace, no womanhood' and is 'the blot and enemy to our general name' (2.3.182–3). Aaron is a 'devil' and Tamora and her sons are 'a pair of cursèd hell-hounds and their dam' (5.2.144).

Lust is seen to draw them together, and indeed 'lust is the only bond, the play suggests, which can possibly join black and white'.[8]

Tamora and Aaron conform to old stereotypes, but in this play such stereotypes highlight the constant renegotiation of national and cultural boundaries. Neither the Goths nor the Romans are pictured as admirable, and Lucius himself is hardly blameless. But, by the end, his alliance with the Goths signals an end to the continuous cycle of violence. He may not be flawless but the play does suggest that he will 'heal Rome's harms and wipe away her woe' (5.3.147). Historically, both Goth and Roman ancestors mingled in England's heritage, and in the play their rift is healed and each side appears more humane, their earlier barbarities obscured by their common revulsion against Tamora and Aaron. Lucius' decision to let the issue of their miscegenation, the black baby, live signals an end to the violence but it cannot be read as a sign of racial tolerance. The baby is a living reminder of the fate of its parents, a symbol of that which both Romans and Goths find most distasteful, and Marcus displays him in order to rally the Romans behind Lucius. The play reminds us that new national identities were being forged in Europe at the same time as external frontiers were opening up, and that domestic realignments were necessary in order to mark off Europe from its 'others'.

The White Devil, or the Politics of Incorporation

Lynda E. Boose has suggested that 'the black man–white female union is, throughout this period and earlier, most frequently depicted as the ultimate romantic-transgressive model of romantic love'.[9] But can it be that this union is revisited by literary texts so often precisely because it is culturally disturbing? Romances, after all encode cultural tensions rather than being just celebratory. Moreover, not all liaisons between black men and white women in this period are visualized as romantic, particularly if the woman is represented as a virago. *Titus Andronicus* (and other plays such as *Lust's Dominion or The Lascivious Queen* which was performed in 1600) suggests that the lust of a black man is corrosive because it mirrors and is fanned by that of an older white woman.

Early modern patriarchal discourses turned upon an opposition between a chaste woman whose sexual appetite is strictly controlled both by her own modesty and by the strict governance of her male kin, and a lusty woman unsupervised by men. In *Titus*, Lavinia conforms to the first type, Tamora embodies the second. It has been suggested that Tamora is 'a particularly vicious representation of a stereotype soon to become a major presence in Jacobean drama—the lusty widow'.[10] It is not clear whether or not Tamora is a widow, but a queen with three sons and no apparent husband would indeed have evoked such a type in the minds of the audience. Tamora's sexuality is especially threatening because she is a powerful older woman: in response to Saturninus' offer of marriage she swears that

> If Saturnine advance the Queen of Goths
> She will be a handmaid to his desires,
> A loving nurse, a mother to his youth.
>
> (1.1.327–9)

Like Shakespeare's Cleopatra, Tamora's sexuality and maternity together threaten a social order which decrees that women should be subordinate to fathers and husbands.

While the spectre of female domination appears to haunt many societies, it cannot be explained away as the result of a trans-historical or universal tension between women and men. Rather, gender relations are an intrinsic part of the social fabric, which gives them their specific form, language, and intensity. Anxiety about female behaviour seems especially acute in times of economic, political, or cultural transformation, and so it is not surprising that, as one historian puts it, there was 'a crisis in gender relations in the years around 1600'.[11] The feminist historian Joan Kelly argued that women's freedom was curtailed rather than enhanced by the so-called Renaissance.[12] Women were pushed out of paying occupations and trade back into the household where their labour became invisible because it was unpaid. Political doctrines, conduct-books, religious tracts as well as other kinds of writings increasingly justified women's subordination to men. The persecution of deviant women escalated and witch-burnings peaked all over Europe. Somewhat contradictorily, though, arguments for women's rights to education and for their equality also became more audible; not only did Europe see a spate of powerful and influential women rulers but arguments for women's freedom and equality were expressed by more ordinary women, and occasionally by some men. Notions of women's inferiority were both challenged and reiterated during this time. These 'gender wars' or 'battle of the sexes' cannot be summarized here, but I want to emphasize that they were also shaped by, and themselves helped shape, ideas about racial difference. Because female independence, sexuality, and political activity help define and delimit cultural boundaries, in Shakespeare's plays, issues of race are always articulated alongside those of appropriate gender roles and sexualities.

Chapter 1 considered how the figure of the Amazon simultaneously expresses racial as well as gender anxieties. Amazons appropriate both the military and the sexual prerogatives of men, warring with as well as seducing them. These seductions are not (as many tales of seduction are) tales of female adoration and surrender; rather, they feature the Amazon's desire to reproduce her community, as in the following story narrated by Montaigne:

When Alexander was passing through Hyracania, Thalestris, queen of the Amazons, came to find him with three hundred warriors of her own sex, well mounted and well armed, having left the remainder of a large army that was following her beyond the neighboring mountains; and said to him, *right out loud and in public*, that the fame of his victories and valor had brought her there to see him, to offer him her resources and power in support of his enterprises; and that finding him so handsome, young and vigorous, she, *who was perfect in all his qualities*, advised him that they should lie together, so that of the most valiant woman in the world and the most valiant man who was then alive, there should be born something great and rare for the future.[13]

Amazonian sexual initiative is particularly frightening because it betrays female political ambitions. In the case of Tamora, as well as Cleopatra and several other transgressive female figures on the Elizabethan and Jacobean stage, the stereotype of the lusty widow is interwoven with that of the Amazon. Lucius calls Tamora a 'most insatiate and luxurious woman' (5.1.88), and even Aaron brands her a 'siren' and 'Semiramis' (an Assyrian queen who was seen to typify female lust). Tamora is not part of an alternative community of women, it is true, and Lavinia accuses her of having 'no womanhood', of being 'the blot and general enemy to our general name' (2.3.182–3). But, like the Amazon, she is a fighting woman who has been subdued in war, who represents a sexual as well as military challenge to the Romans, and seeks to reinstate a hierarchy where she will reign.

The Amazon has to be both captured and husbanded: the effective husbanding and 'taming' of a foreign queen was important in a society where alliances between different clans and nations were secured by the exchange of women. The ability of women to adapt to their new homes was essential to the security and stability of this process. In this context, female duplicity also takes on an added significance, for it can signify women's secret resistance to being assimilated. In *A Midsummer Night's Dream*, the Amazon Hippolyta seems to comply with Theseus's will, but critics have pointed out that she does not endorse his opinions and appears less enthusiastic about their approaching marriage than he is. In *Titus*, one Roman subdues Tamora in war, while another marries her. Saturninus' ineffectuality as a king is underlined by his inability to control, or even interpret Tamora. Although Tamora pretends to be the compliant wife, her duplicity is clear to the audience who knows that it threatens the stability of the Roman state. If the chaste Lavinia is symbolic of Rome, as critics often suggest, the lusty Tamora represents the threat to the city's civility, a threat that is especially dangerous because it has lodged itself in the heart of Rome. She is, as she slyly reminds Titus, 'incorporate in Rome | A Roman now adopted happily' (1.1.459–60).

The Romans consistently use sexual double entendre to describe Tamora. In the opening scene, Marcus wants to know how 'the subtle Queen of Goths' has so suddenly 'advanced in Rome' and Titus says he does not know whether or not 'device' or cunning has brought her to this 'high good turn' (1.1.389–394). 'Turn' was a word used for the sexual act, apart from its implications of changeability, a quality frequently attributed to unchaste women. Desdemona too, we may recall, is accused in similar terms by Othello: she 'can turn, and turn, and yet go on | And turn again…' (4.1.255–6). Daniel Vitkus has pointed out that religious conversion and sexual perversion were both implied in the verb 'to turn'; the phrase 'to turn Turk', for example, carried erotic connotations which drew upon ideas of Muslim hyper-sexuality as well as female immorality.[14] Thus Tamora brings together widespread fears of outsiders, particularly converts, with the anxieties surrounding duplicitous women and foreign queens.

Titus Andronicus, along with many others of Shakespeare's plays, registers the ways in which emergent ideologies of race complicate feudal alliances and warfare, and it does so obliquely by aligning dangerous femininity with blackness. Tamora's duplicity is most spectacularly manifested in her liaison with the black Aaron. And it is her black child who most powerfully signals the dangers of female deviance and threatens her 'incorporation' and assimilation in Rome. Her son Demetrius points out that the child, whom the nurse describes as 'a devil', a 'joyless, dismal, black and sorrowful issue' that is 'as loathsome as a toad' (4.2.64–7), will expose Tamora in the way a white child would never have done: 'by this our mother is for ever shamed' (4.2.111). Lucius regards the baby as the 'base fruit of her burning lust' (5.1.43). Tamora, the unnatural mother, wants the child killed, and Chiron and Demetrius endorse this decision. But of course, as Aaron points out to them, this is their brother. The relationship underscores the play's equation between morality and blackness: Chiron and Demetrius' debased nature is kin to blackness, just as their mother is the natural partner to Aaron. At the same time, the idea that white and black folk can be related by blood (an idea that was not inconceivable in the medieval romance *Parzival*) would have been horrifying to early modern English audiences.

Renaissance writings reiterated the belief that blackness can overpower as well as contaminate whiteness: Reginald Scot's *The Discoverie of Witchcraft* (1584) warned its readers told that 'In truth a black Moore never faileth to beget blacke children, of what colour soever the other be'.[15] Aaron suggests that this need not always be true, and says to Tamora's sons that 'one Muliteus my countryman' and his white wife have produced a child 'like to her, fair as you are' (4.2.151–3). He proposes substituting that child for his own. Critics have generally assumed that Aaron fabricates this story. Eldred Jones comments that had it been true, 'there is no reason why he should not have carried out the manoeuvre of exchanging the two children with his customary despatch. Instead, as soon as he has successfully quietened the fears of Demetrius and Chiron with his tale, and has sent them to bury the nurse, he reveals a completely different plan' of spiriting away his black child and bringing it up 'in a cave . . . | To be a warrior and command a camp' (4.3.178–9).[16] Aaron is of course a habitual liar, but he has never talked about *exchanging* the two children, only that the white child shall be

> substituted in the place of mine,
> To calm this tempest whirling in the court;
> And let the Emperor dandle him for his own.

(4.2.158–60)

We do not know whether this ever happens but certainly there is no 'tempest' in the court, no scandal about the empress having given birth to a black child and no report of a stillborn or dead child. Therefore it is as reasonable to assume that such a substitution has taken place as it is to surmise that Aaron is lying.

The news of the black child reaches the Goths and Lucius through Aaron himself, who is overheard by one of them talking to his child, and the Romans learn of its existence from Lucius, but only after Saturninus is dead. Lucius has promised Aaron the child will live, and at the end of the play he does not retract this promise, although we do not know what will become of it. Both Tamora and Aaron will die, but the scandal of their illicit liaison will survive through the child. This is the only interracial child in Shakespeare's plays, and it is so disturbing an idea that the play cannot discuss his fate or place in a cleaned up Rome. Critics have long commented that Aaron's defence of his child humanizes him. Titus is willing to kill his own children in order to honour his principles; Tamora can think of having this child murdered in order to protect her honour: only Aaron puts his child's life above his own. As Eldred Jones comments, Aaron's 'defence of his child is also his defence of his colour'. The child prompts him to question whether black is 'so base a hue' and to defend the steadfast nature of blackness, its inability to be washed white. In fact it is whiteness that is weaker and betrayed by blushes, or overcome by blackness, just as Tamora's colour is overwhelmed by Aaron's in their baby. Thus Aaron's pride in his child is pride in his colour as well as in his paternity; for him, as much as for the white Romans, race is indeed lineage.

Othello *and the Racial Question*

Othello is both a fantasy of interracial love and social tolerance, and a nightmare of racial hatred and male violence. In this play, a white woman flouts the established social hierarchies of 'clime, complexion and degree' to marry a black man, an act that betrays, in the eyes of some beholders, 'Foul disproportions, thoughts unnatural!' (3.3.235–8). Location, skin colour, and class are seen to add up to 'nature' itself. But the real tragedy of the play lies in the fact that these hierarchies are not external to the pair. Iago's machinations are effective because Othello is predisposed to believing his pronouncements about the inherent duplicity of women, and the necessary fragility of an 'unnatural' relationship between a young, white, well-born woman and an older black soldier. Ideologies, the play tells us, only work because they are not entirely external to us. Othello is a victim of racial beliefs precisely because he becomes an agent of misogynist ones.

The portrayal of Othello, the 'Moor of Venice' stands at the complicated crux of contemporary beliefs about black people and Muslims. As we have seen, black-skinned people were usually typed as godless, bestial, and hideous, fit only to be saved (and in early modern Europe, enslaved) by Christians. On the other hand, commentators such as Henry Blount wondered whether Muslims, with their tightly organized religion and sophisticated empires, were 'absolutely barbarous' or whether they had 'another kind of civility, different from ours'.[1] Both blacks and Muslims were regarded as given to unnatural sexual and domestic practices, as highly emotional and even irrational, and prone to anger and jealousy; above all, both existed outside the Christian fold. *Othello* yokes together and reshapes available images of 'blackamoors' and Moors, giving us a black Moor who has both a slave past and a noble lineage, a black skin and thick lips as well as great military skill and rhetorical abilities, a capacity for tenderness as well as a propensity to violence.

This cocktail has provoked fierce debates about Othello's appearance and racial origins. Various characters in the play (including himself) harp upon his 'sooty bosom' and his 'thick lips'; recalling age-old stereotypes of black people, they call him 'a devil', 'old black ram', and 'a Barbary horse', all images which attached to sub-Saharan Africans. But the 'lascivious Moor' with his 'sword of Spain' also evokes the image of the 'turbaned Turk' to whom he compares himself at the end of the play. Did Shakespeare picture Othello like the slightly menacing turbaned and aristocratic figure shown in a contemporary picture (Fig. 6)? In an earlier period, critics who wanted to rescue Shakespeare's hero from the taint of blackness were eager to prove that even if dark or 'African', in Shakespeare's imagination, Othello could not possibly be 'Negroid'. Today, his blackness often gets underplayed by those who want to draw our attention to the Muslim aspects of the 'Moor' or emphasized at their expense. Thus there is a real difficulty in deciding whether Othello's tragedy has to do with his being a 'circumcised dog' or his having a 'sooty bosom'.

I suggest that it is impossible, but also unnecessary, to decide whether Othello is *more* or *less* 'African'/'black' than 'Turkish'/ Muslim. Turks and Muslims were often regarded as both morally and physically darker than Christians, and some dark-skinned Africans were also Muslims. A picture of a noble Moor in Cesare Vecellio's sixteenth-century book of costumes shows a man with turban, flowing robes, and a sword, with thick lips and a dark skin (Fig. 7). This picture tells us that despite the physical difference between most Spanish Moors and most sub-Saharan Africans, a more composite figure was imaginable. Since there were also fair Muslims and black non-Muslims, however, we should not simply explain away the tension between these different aspects of Othello. Instead of simply corresponding to any particular historically identifiable group of black Muslims, Othello indicates the way in which medieval as well as newer ideas about blacks and Muslims intersected in early modern England. He is, as Dympna Callaghan points out, the representation of an idea of the Moor, and such an idea does not simply

MORO DI CONDI-TIONE.

7. Moor of Quality from Cesare Vecellio, *Degli habiti antichi et moderne...*

reflect historical reality but mediates it.[2] More than any other play of the time, *Othello* allows us to see that skin colour, religion, and location were often contradictorily yoked together within ideologies of 'race', and that all of these attributes were animated by notions of sexual and gender difference.

The Jealous Moor

Early modern accounts of the East, and especially Turkey, were obsessed with its supposed sensuality, as well as by its imperial might. These two qualities were sometimes regarded as antithetical to one another, and at other times as complementary. 'Jealousy' was a term that was applicable in both public and private spheres— Robert Burton's *Anatomy of Melancholy* informed its readers that Turks were prone to 'jealous outrages' of the political kind, and cited many examples where Turks brutally eliminated their rivals.[3] The political and the familial spheres were closely intertwined in the Ottoman Empire. Richard Knolles, whose popular and enormously influential *General History of the Turks* (1603) was consulted by Shakespeare while writing *Othello,* described murders within the royal family, with rulers killing their brothers, cousins, and even sons to thwart any political opposition. These books also detailed instances of Turkish sexual jealousies and strict control over women's lives, implying that sexual and political power were somehow interrelated. Robert Burton cites various authorities to make his point:

Southern men are more hot, lascivious and jealous, than such as live in the North: they can hardly contain themselves in those hotter climes, but are the most subject to prodigious lusts. Leo Afer telleth incredible things almost of the lust and jealousy of his Countrymen of Africa, and especially such as live about Carthage, and so doth every Geographer of them in Asia, Turkey, Spain, Italy. Germany hath not so many drunkards, England Tobacconists, France Dancers, Holland Mariners, as Italy alone hath jealous husbands.... (827)

Hence, lust and jealousy as well as black skin are the result of a hot climate. We see too that lands in Southern Europe coalesce with those East or south of Europe to create a general category, 'Southern' which includes, among other locations, Africa, Turkey, Spain, and Italy, and is distinguished from a Northern Englishness.

Othello is partly set in Italy, a setting that in Shakespeare's plays both reflects, and offers a contrast to, the audience's England. Italians are 'Southern' like the Asians, different from the English, but when placed against the Moors, they are part of Christian Europe. Othello, 'the Moor of Venice' is a Moor who cannot fully become a part of Venice. His jealousy is rooted in this fact and in his difference from Desdemona, a difference that Iago plays upon in order to persuade Othello that his wife cannot really love him for very long. In Giraldi Cinthio's *Gli Hecatommithi,* from which Shakespeare took the story of the unhappy marriage of a Moor and a Venetian lady, Disdemona tells her husband, 'you Moors are so hot by nature that any little thing moves you to anger and revenge'. Shakespeare has his Desdemona counter this stereotype; when Emilia asks her, 'Is he not jealous?' she replies 'Who, he? I think the sun where he was born | Drew all such humours from him' (3.4.28–30). But the play goes on to show us that, despite his seeming different from other Moors, Othello ultimately embodies the stereotype of Moorish lust and violence—a jealous, murderous husband of a Christian lady.

Stories of a Turkish emperor or general loving and then killing a beautiful Christian woman circulated freely in early modern England. William Painter's *The Palace of Pleasure* (1567) recounts that Hyerenee, a beautiful Greek, was murdered by Mahomet, 'the barbarous cruel Prince', because his passion for her distracted him from his duties as emperor. Mahomet kills Hyerenee before his assembled court, and asks his audience, 'Now ye know, whether or not your Emperor is able to repress and bridle his affection or not?'[4] Richard Knolles's *History of the Turks* (1603) narrates another version of this story, in which Irene becomes 'the mistress and commander' of the great conqueror Sultan Mahomet.[5] The Sultan's love changes him: 'his fierce nature was now by her tamed, and his wonted care of arms quite neglected: Mars slept in Venus lap' (350). Upon being rebuked by his adviser Mustapha Bassa, he is torn between his military duty and his love—'he was at war with himself'—a conflict that he resolves by killing Irene (352–3). Knolles also tells the story of yet another Greek lady called Manto, who was loved by the Turkish general Ionuses Bassa. The general, 'more amorous of her person than secured in her virtues, and after the manner of sensual men' soon 'began to have her in distrust, although he saw no great cause why'. His 'mad humour' grows to such an extent that when Manto attempts to escape, he kills her (557–9).

Shakespeare knew some of these texts and whether or not *Othello* was directly inspired by any of them, it certainly reworks their motif of a Muslim soldier who loves a Christian woman 'not wisely but too well'. Like Knolles's Irene, Desdemona has become 'our great captain's captain' (2.1.75), and Othello's jealousy, like Mahomet's, puts him 'at war with himself'; like Ionuses Bassa too, he torments himself and his loved one. Unlike these other figures, however, Othello is not unmanned by his love for his 'fair warrior' (although Iago suggests precisely this to him). Rather, it is the erosion of his love that threatens to take away his 'occupation' and bring 'chaos' upon him. Shakespeare also goes to greater lengths than Knolles to map the sexual drama upon the racial and cultural one, making one hinge upon the other. The jealousy that tears Othello apart manifests itself as a division between his Christian, loving, rational self, and the Muslim identity that erupts and disrupts it.

Turkish harems were reputed to be filled with beautiful Christian girls captured to satisfy what John Foxe's *Acts and Monuments* condemned as 'most filthy villainy of the bestial Turks'.[6] The Sultana Valide, wife of the Sultan Amurath III, was a Venetian woman of the house of Basso and was captured when young. Foxe, Knolles, and other writers also claimed that Turkish strongmen or Janizzaries were captured Christian men who were forcibly converted to Islam, and they described at length the misery, hunger, tortures, and indignities suffered by male as well as female captives. Thanks to the aggressive Turkish policy of converting Christians, says Foxe, 'there are few now remaining, which are Turks indeed by birth and blood'; the Turkish Empire is therefore upheld 'by the strength and power of soldiers which have been Christians, and now turned to Mahumet's religion, so that even their own natural language is now out of use among them' (964). Othello's story counters these tales. If Turkish warriors are really converted Christians, Othello the converted Moor will halt the menacing advance of the Turks, the latest in a long line of 'wicked Saracens' who, as Fox put it, 'in the space of thirty years, subdued Arabia, got Valencia, Phenicia, Syria, Egypt and Persia, and not long after they proceeded further and got Africa, and then Asia' (964).

But religious conversion speaks as much to a crisis of identity as to a triumph of self-fashioning. Foxe's statement that the Turks who threaten Europe are really converted Christians implies that race and culture can be acquired and shed. At the same time, Foxe also marks out Muslims as Satan's agents who are empowered by 'dissention and discord' among Christians, and suggests that the struggle between Christians and Turks is as eternal as that between good and evil. *Othello* responds to these anxieties about the nature of ethnic, racial, and religious identity. While Othello is the defender of the Christian state against the Muslim threat, he also embodies this threat. At the end of the play, he describes his suicide as an act where his Christian half kills the Muslim half, much as long ago in Aleppo, he had killed 'a malignant and turbaned Turk', a 'circumcised dog' who had beaten 'a Venetian and traduced the state' (5.2.361–3). Despite being a Christian soldier, Othello cannot shed either his blackness or his 'Turkish' attributes, and it is his sexual and emotional self, expressed through his relationship with Desdemona, which interrupts and finally disrupts his newly acquired Christian and Venetian identity. In the eyes of many Venetians, he remains illegitimate as Desdemona's suitor; as her husband, he seems fated to play out the script of jealousy and wife-murder.

The Infidelity of Women

In trying to understand the complex ways in which *Othello* plays upon racial and cultural difference, it is important to note that admiration as well as revulsion were both part of English reports about the tight political and sexual control of the Turks over their various subjects. One account of the Turkomanni people can barely hide its envy of the people whose wives 'spend their time in spinning, carding, knitting, or some household housewifery, not spending their time in gossiping or gadding abroad from place to place, and from house to house; from ale-house to tavern, as many wives in England do'. Describing the segregation of the sexes and the strict policing of women, it goes on:

If the like order were in England, women would be more dutiful and faithful to their husbands than they are for there if a man have a hundred women, if any one of them prostitute herself to any man but her own husband, he hath authority to bind her, hands and feet, and cast her unto a river, with a stone about her neck, and drown her. . . .[7]

We have seen that Othello's jealous violence reinforces stereotypes of 'Southern' men, but it is also crucial to note that Iago stokes and manipulates this violence by evoking equally commonplace images of women's duplicity. In fact, Iago does not believe Othello is the jealous type—'The Moor... | Is of a constant, loving, noble nature' he says (2.1.287–8). But this 'nature', he believes, can be transformed and returned to the stereotype of the jealous Turk by harping upon female inconstancy. When they arrive at Cyprus, Iago tells Desdemona that women are

> pictures out of door,
> Bells in your parlours; wildcats in your kitchens,
> Saints in your injuries; devils being offended,
> Players in your housewifery, and hussies in your beds.

(2.1.112–15)

This banter simply underlines what many men in the play believe about women. Brabanzio has already cautioned Othello: 'Look to her, Moor, if thou has eyes to see. | She has deceived her father, and may thee' (1.3.292–3). Iago practically echoes these lines: 'She did deceive her father, marrying you, | And when she seemed to shake and fear your looks | She loved them most' (3.3.210–12). He warns Othello against 'the green-eyed monster' who consumes those men who expect fidelity from their wives, whereas 'That cuckold lives in bliss | Who, certain of his fate, loves not his wronger' (171–2). Those who know that all wives are potentially unfaithful arm themselves by not loving them too much.

Robert Burton also informed readers of his *Anatomy of Melancholy* that men who dote excessively on their wives are 'too effeminate' and likely to be jealous, and that this sentiment was especially 'evident in old men.... All wives are slippery, often unfaithful to their husbands...but to old men most treacherous'. Finally, 'A fourth eminent cause of jealousy may be this, when he that is deformed, as Pindar says of Vulcan, without natural graces...will marry some fair nice piece.... Can she be fair and honest too?' (832). Written after *Othello*, Burton's *Anatomy* could not have been an inspiration for the play but in fact may well have been influenced by it. Moreover, the overlap between the two texts indicates the nature of contemporary beliefs about both masculinity and jealousy, especially as Burton draws freely upon other texts and commentaries. It is striking that Iago harps upon all the causes of jealousy enumerated by Burton— Othello's excessive love for Desdemona, the enormous disparities of age, culture, and race between them, and women's propensity to stray. Whereas Othello had once believed that he had no cause for jealousy because Desdemona 'had eyes and chose me', he now echoes Iago:

> Haply for I am black,
> And have not those soft parts of conversation
> That chamberers have; or for I am declined
> Into the vale of years—yet that's not much—
> She's gone. I am abused, and my relief
> Must be to loathe her. O curse of marriage,
> That we can call these delicate creatures ours
> And not their appetites!
>
> (3.3.267–74)

There run two common threads in Brabanzio's, Iago's, and Othello's lines—first, that this match is unusual, 'unnatural', and therefore especially fragile, and second, that women are inconstant and deceitful. Whether Othello imbibes these beliefs from Iago, or Iago only plays upon what Othello already believes, the point is that for all of them male jealousy hinges upon racial difference as well as upon female infidelity.

Italian, and especially Venetian, women were reputed to be particularly licentious. Iago tells Othello:

> In Venice they do let God see the pranks
> They dare not show their husbands; their best conscience
> Is not to leave't undone, but keep't unknown.
>
> (3.3.206–8)

Contemporary writings suggested that Italian women were 'very lewd and wicked, for even in the ancient city of Rome, there are many thousands of lewd living women that pay monthly unto the Pope for the sinful use of their wicked bodies'.[8] Venice was repeatedly pictured as a city full of whores, and it was often personified as one. Certainly the theatre made full use of this idea. Written some years after *Othello*, Webster's play *The White Devil* (1612) featured 'The Life and Death of Vittoria Corombona, the famous Venetian Courtezan'. In that play, Vittoria (who is adulterous but not a prostitute) spiritedly challenges the men who label her a 'whore'. But Desdemona is stunned when Othello asks her—'Are you not a strumpet? . . . not a whore? . . . I took you for that cunning whore of Venice | That married with Othello' (4.2.84–94). She can barely bring herself to repeat the word 'whore': 'Am I that name, Iago?' (4.2.121). Iago himself has called Desdemona a 'super-subtle Venetian' (2.1.355). Of course, the audience knows that she is honest but by evoking these beliefs the play also suggests that perhaps Othello can be forgiven for thinking that Desdemona might be straying. This ambiguity is at the heart of the play—any sympathy for Othello reinforces the misogynist sentiments mouthed by some characters, and any sympathy for Desdemona endorses the view that Othello is a 'gull, a dolt, a devil'. Here, it is sexual politics that gives racial and cultural differences their cultural meanings and effect.

There are only three women in *Othello*—Bianca, who is treated as a whore, Desdemona, who is repeatedly accused of being one, and Emilia, who is dismissed as her 'bawd'. The charge of sexual impropriety haunts each one of them, and Desdemona and Emilia are murdered by their husbands. I have suggested that English stories of patriarchal violence in Muslim cultures served both to define the incivility of these cultures and to offer models for domestic control of unruly women. Burton repeats a picture common in many travelogues:

The Turks have I know not how many black deformed eunuchs ... to this purpose sent commonly from Egypt, deprived in their childhood of all their privities, and brought up in the Seraglio at Constantinople, to keep their wives; which are so penned up they may not confer with any living man, or converse with younger women, have a cucumber or carrot sent in to them for their diet, but sliced, for fear. ... I have not said all, they not only lock them up, but lock up their private parts ... certain tribes ... sew up the parts of female infants at birth, leaving a way for the urine, and when they grow up, give them in marriage thus sewn up, so that it is the husband's first business to cut apart the fettered nether lips of the maiden. (843–4)

Burton claims that Muscovites are as jealous as ancient Gauls, and concludes that ' 'Twas well performed and ordered by the Greeks, that a matron should not be seen in public without her husband to speak for her ... For a woman abroad and alone is like a deer broke out of a park, whom every hunter follows' (863). Thus control of women is the defining feature of cultural otherness, but the divide between 'us' and 'them' mutates into a gender divide, so that horrific foreign practices become the basis for prescribing gender roles at home.

Burton writes that Jews and Africans 'will not credit virginity without seeing the bloody napkin'; like other writers of the period,

Burton gets this and many other stories from the enormously successful *History and Description of Africa* which was written in 1526 by a real-life Moorish convert, Al-Hassan Ibn Mohammed Al-Wezaa, Al-Fazi, known to his readers as Leo Africanus, or Leo Afer. This book was often reprinted during the sixteenth century. Four years before *Othello* was written, it was translated into English by John Pory, and long excerpts were reproduced in Samuel Purchas's travel collection *Hakluytus Posthumus*. Many English writers used Africanus to bolster their own opinions of Africans, Muslims, and women, and his descriptions of African women who 'pleasure' one another as well as of clitoral excision became central to Western medical discourse and its constructions of deviant female sexuality. In *Othello*, the same handkerchief shows up, this time not bloody with virginal blood but a napkin whose loss stands in for the 'ocular proof' of Desdemona's lack of chastity. Othello is both the jealous African and the Venetian husband watching out for the 'pranks' that Venetian wives 'dare not show their husbands'.[9] Africanus's book was widely seen as an 'insider's' scoop on Africa, and it reinforced several stereotypes about the Moors, including that of jealousy: 'No nation in the world is so subject unto jealousy; for they will rather lose their lives, than put up any disgrace in behalf of their women.'[10] Africanus suggests that such jealousy is an index of political and cultural sophistication, remarking that the more highly developed societies of that continent displayed male jealousy, whereas the more brutish kinds of people in Africa let their women roam like uncontrolled animals. The words 'liberal' and 'jealous' are constantly juxtaposed in his book, infusing an element of admiration for the jealous Moor.

Such narratives help us to gauge the various ways in which *Othello* might have played upon the beliefs, anxieties, or desires of its audiences. Desdemona not only disobeys her father and chooses her own husband, she defends her choice in front of the Senate, openly affirming her sexual passion for Othello. As I have suggested elsewhere, Desdemona's passion needs to be articulated explicitly because its object is black, but such articulation makes it especially transgressive and disturbing.[11] If she was 'half the wooer' then Othello cannot be a magician who has illegitimately charmed her, as Brabanzio suggests. The white daughter has not been raped but actively desires the black man. But Desdemona rewrites her transgression in terms of ordinary familial patterns, pointing out that breaking away from a father is necessary in order to cleave to a husband:

> I do perceive here divided duty.
> To you I am bound for life and education.
>
> .   .   .   .   .
>
>   You are the lord of duty,
> I am hitherto your daughter. But here's my husband,
> And so much duty as my mother showed
> To you, preferring you before her father,
> So much I challenge that I may profess
> Due to the Moor my lord.
>
>   (1.3.180–8)

Desdemona's affirmation of desire is cleverly articulated in the language of wifely obedience, ignoring the fact that Othello's colour alters the usual scenario of female transitions from one man to another.

On the Renaissance stage, lovers who challenge familial authority are usually romanticized, even if they ultimately meet a tragic fate. But married (even widowed) women who disobey their husbands (or other male figures of authority) are usually punished, even if these men are tyrannical. Critics have argued that the plays thus help propagate a new ideal of 'companionate marriage' in which romance is not antithetical to matrimony, but women's chastity and obedience are still crucial. Assertions such as this—'England is a paradise for women, and hell for horses: Italy a paradise for horses, a hell for women'—were double-edged, at once confirming English superiority over more rigid cultures, and barely masking an anxiety about female unruliness. Thus Desdemona's free banter with Iago and her spirited defence of Cassio, although innocent, stages a model of behaviour that was controversial in the culture at large. So does Emilia's outspokenness, even though it is her submission to her husband, and not her defiance, which allows the handkerchief to be used as evidence against Desdemona. It is hard to conclude whether violence against outspoken or transgressive women on the stages of the time had the effect of reinforcing patriarchal attitudes to women, or of unsettling them. The effects of stage narratives are likely to have been diverse, tapping as they did into a wide spectrum of changing beliefs about gender roles. It is even harder to assume that all audiences, who included both men and women of different classes, would have responded uniformly to stage characters such as Desdemona and Emilia. However, the point is that such figures speak to widespread contemporary anxieties and debates about appropriate female behaviour, and in Desdemona's case the question of wifely submission is especially complex because the husband is a Moor. For all their heterogeneity in terms of class and gender, *Othello*'s original audiences and actors would have been mostly English and entirely white.

Venice, Spain, and Turkey

The English saw Venice not simply as a place for female deviance, but also as an ideal republic and hub of international trade. Whereas female 'openness' was dangerous and immoral, political and mercantile openness was much admired by an England in search of overseas markets and colonies. Despite its Catholicism, Venice became an ideal that was invoked by English writers subtly to critique domestic affairs. In 1599, Lewis Lewknor translated into English Contarini's *Commonwealth and Government of Venice*, a work with which Shakespeare was familiar.[12] This book helped propagate a 'myth of Venice' in England which exalted the city-state as an open but ordered society, a model of civility which informs Brabanzio's angry assertion: 'This is Venice. | My house is not a grange' (1.1.107–8). Brabanzio's choice of words is ironic, for Iago tells him that in fact his house *has* become a grange in which a 'black ram', a 'Barbary horse' is 'tupping' his daughter (1.1.88, 89, 113). Venetian civility has been built by letting in the very foreigners who now threaten to undermine it at a different level. Because Othello is needed in order to combat the Turks, the Senate is willing to regard him as 'more fair than black' but for Desdemona's father such colour-blindness is not possible. Here we see a tension between the state and the family, although the two were so often equated in contemporary political rhetoric.

How might an English audience have reacted to the Senate's pronouncements? As discussed earlier, England was increasingly hostile to foreigners, both officially and at a popular level, and London had witnessed several major riots against foreign residents and artisans. Would this play have unsettled or reinforced such hostility?

Did the play make the case for a tolerant society, or did it issue a warning not only to disobedient daughters but also to 'open societies' who let in outsiders, especially black ones? It might be useful to recall that if some English writers extolled the virtues of Venice, others found Italy a dangerous model for the English: 'the religion, the learning, the policy, the experience, the manner of Italy' were the 'enchantments of Circe, brought out of Italy, to mar men's manners in England'.[13] Thus Venice's openness could also be viewed as dangerous by a society itself fairly suspicious of outsiders.

Some critics have suggested that Shakespeare's audience was in fact quite tolerant of Moors, and that *Othello* capitalizes on this tolerance to criticize Spain, where Christians had warred with Moors for centuries.[14] Spanish conflicts are crucial for understanding the racial consciousness of early modern Europe, and Iago's hatred of Othello definitely invokes the hostility of the Old Christians in Spain towards the newly converted Moors there. Iago's name recalls the patron saint of Spain, Sant Iago, or Saint James, who was known as Santiago Matamoros, St James the Moor-killer.[15] Hatred of Catholic Spain was a defining feature of Protestant England, who sought to define its own empire in opposition to that of Spain. Eric Griffin points to the fact that England was looking to establish mercantile and diplomatic relations with Muslim countries and that many English commentators suggested that Protestants and Muslims were alike in their hatred of both idol-worship and Catholics: 'Spain's national obsession with purity of blood', he concludes 'had met its ideological reverse in an English Protestant obsession with purity of faith' (82). This is in many ways a persuasive argument, and it is particularly valuable in insisting that we think about England not as an isolated unit but in relation to other European nations and colonial models. But can we then conclude, as Griffin does, that by demonizing Iago, *Othello* is indicting *only* Spanish racism and suggesting English tolerance?

The diplomatic flirting and mercantile exchanges between the English and the Turks and Moroccans cannot be isolated from a long and complicated history of ambivalence regarding Islam—attitudes to Muslims, especially Turks, were contradictory and complicated rather than simply admiring or simply negative. In fact I want to suggest that political and commercial desires to establish traffic with Muslim powers exacerbated prevalent tensions and anxieties about religious and cultural difference. If on the one hand references were made to the shared Protestant and Muslim hatred of Spain and 'idolatry', then, on the other, English anti-Catholicism was often articulated by suggesting a continuum rather than a difference between Muslim infidels and Catholics. John Foxe's *Acts and Monuments* argues that Turks are rampant all over Asia because of the 'dissension and discord, falsehood and idleness' that have spread among Christians. Thus, false Christianity such as Catholicism opens the door to Turks; the enemy is enabled by that which we 'nourish within our breasts' at home (964–5). Of course, Catholics in Spain and elsewhere argued exactly the opposite—that Protestants were the 'sect of Mahumette'; thus both sides regarded Muslims as 'only the whip with the which the holy and righteous Lord doth beat and scourge us for our own vicious living'.[16] Rather than representing clear English admiration of a group that was hated in Spain, *Othello* plays upon these ambiguities and contradictions about the Moors that intersected with schisms within Christianity.

Moreover, the history of Spanish blood laws tells us that the idea of purity of blood was not counterposed to, but measured by purity of faith. As we have seen, these two concepts were linked by the Inquisition, and by authorities in Spain and elsewhere. Conversion was officially required of Jews and Moors, yet it was culturally frightening precisely because it called into question the boundary between insider and outsider. That is why this boundary was increasingly defined in quasi-biological terms. An 'Old Christian' was now regarded as different in 'blood' from a new convert. Religious conversions also signal the possibility of a reverse traffic whereby Christians convert to another faith, another identity, and this was a pervasive fear all over Europe. Thus by linking faith to blood, the Christian authorities were also suggesting that 'turning Turk' was only a superficial exercise. This is precisely the dynamic that Shakespeare plays upon in both *Othello* and *The Merchant of Venice*, where Moors and Jews are dangerous precisely because they are 'of Venice', and where that danger is mirrored by the possibility that Christian maidens will become part of alien households.

Such anxieties were not confined to Spain. After their official expulsion in 1290, Jews could only live as converts in England, and yet, as James Shapiro shows, Elizabethan England was still beset by anxieties about Jews that were heightened by events in Spain. Moors did not have the same long history of presence within England and the English tended to associate them with locations such as Turkey, Spain, Morocco, Persia, India, and parts of Africa. But widespread stories of Christians turning Turk brought the Moors closer home. Christian conversions to Islam were part of Crusading lore, and were also narrated as an essential feature of the Turkish Empire. Most urgently, though, they were seen as an alarming feature of the growing English trade with Ottoman and North African territories.

In a recent essay, Julia Reinhard Lupton evokes Christian/Muslim tensions to offer an argument that is the exact opposite of Griffin's. For her, a Muslim Othello would have been far more dangerous in the eyes of English audiences than a black Othello. A black Othello, Lupton suggests, is analogous to the uncivilized American or Caliban, a barbaric figure outside all religion and therefore more easily convertible to Christianity. A Muslim or Turkish Othello on the other hand is less convertible because he already owes allegiance to a rival religion of the book.[17] Lupton argues that critics have imposed upon the play the horror of 'monstrous miscegenation' which was a feature of the nineteenth-century racial imagination. In the Renaissance, she concludes, a black Gentile could be legitimately placed within the narrative of an international romance, in a way that the Infidel Turk could not: 'whereas for the modern reader or viewer a black Othello is more subversive, "other", or dangerous, in the Renaissance scene a paler Othello more closely resembling the Turks whom he fights might actually challenge more deeply the integrity of the Christian paradigms set up in the play as a measure of humanity' (74).

Lupton is right in asking us to place *Othello* within Christian Islamophobia, but I suggest that the play responds to contemporary tensions about religious difference precisely by complicating them with the question of skin colour. If on the one hand the lack of colour difference provoked acute anxieties about conversions in Europe, on the other, as discussed in Chapter 2, blackness posed different, but no less acute, misgivings about this process. It is Othello's colour that provokes anxieties about Othello's integration into Venice—Iago, Brabanzio, and Roderigo do not worry that Othello will assimilate unnoticed, but that he will produce, with a white woman, spectacular evidence of miscegenation. In fact, the power of this play is that it brings blackness and religious difference into simultaneous play while also making visible the tensions between them.

Othello, Africanus, and Moorish Difference

Such mingling is also evident in Africanus's *History of Africa* which Shakespeare drew upon for his ideas of Moorish jealousy but also Moorish capacity for learning and military skill. The French writer Jean Bodin described Africanus himself as 'by descent a More, born in Spain, in religion a Mahumetan, and afterward a Christian, having by continual journeys travelled almost over all Africa; as also over all Asia minor, and a good part of Europe, was taken by certain pirates, and presented to Pope Leo the tenth'.[18] Othello narrates a similar tale of travel and captivity, and both Othello and Africanus establish themselves among Christians by narrating these stories. John Pory, Africanus's translator, marvelled 'much how he should have escaped so many thousands of imminent dangers', just as Othello tells the Senate that Desdemona loved him for his stories of 'dangers I had passed' (1.3.166). Africanus affirms his adaptability, claiming that he is like a 'most wily bird' called Amphibia, who would continually 'change her element' from air to water in order to avoid paying taxes to the king of birds as well as to the king of fishes. 'For mine own part', Africanus writes, when I hear the Africans evil spoken of, I will affirm myself to be one of Granada: and when I perceive the nation of Granada to be discommended, then I will profess myself to be an African' (190). Othello also mimics Venetian and Christian discourse to his own advantage, and strategically invokes his non-Venetian lineage and history when it suits him. Finally, Othello and Africanus also share another rhetorical strategy—Shakespeare's hero consolidates his own position in Venice by establishing his distance from cannibals and monsters whom he has overcome, and Turks whom he has fought and will continue to combat; similarly, Africanus establishes himself as a reliable historiographer by reproducing dominant notions about dark-skinned 'negroes' as well as African women.

Most critics regard Africanus's narrative as consolidating ideas of difference between Africans and Europeans by establishing his authority as an eyewitness who was once one of 'them' but now has crossed over to 'us'. But Jonathan Burton rightly points out that Africanus also destabilizes some of these binary oppositions by asserting Moorish learning and achievement, by citing Muslim scholars, and by presenting Africans as a heterogeneous group of peoples with different lifestyles, achievements, and attributes.[19] Sometimes Africanus explicitly challenges European understanding of Africa, pointing out that they mispronounce the Arabic El Chahira as 'Cairo' (870) and harp upon Carthage's classical links with the story of Dido and Aeneas rather than seeing it as a modern complex city (715–16). However, Africanus manages to complicate received opinions about North African civilizations as well as lighter-skinned Muslim men only by reinforcing their distance from 'Negroes' and women. Burton also asks us not to collapse the historical figure Africanus into the literary hero, Othello. Both establish their own status by distancing themselves from people with whom Europeans could confuse them but whereas Othello cannot sustain his strategy and falls prey to the dominant discourse about Muslims and blacks, Africanus's text succeeds in establishing its claim to impartiality. For over 200 years, it was widely considered to be an objective and accurate account of 'Africa'.

This crucial difference between Othello and Africanus takes us back to the question of skin colour. Pory, Bodin, and other early modern commentators on Africanus draw attention to his being both a 'More and a Mahumetane in religion' (Africanus, *History*, 6). This seems to imply that Africanus, like Othello, was black as well as a Muslim. Given his Spanish origins, it is likely that his skin colour was dark in relation to Northern Europeans, but lighter than that of sub-Saharan Africans. Whatever his own colour, Africanus's *History* suggests that fairer Moors are more civilized than darker ones, and are therefore more translatable both into European codes of civility and the Christian faith. In his entire history of Africa, references to the civility of black people are rare; for the most part Africanus either ignores the non-Islamic sections of Africa or presents them as brutish. If, while discussing Barbary, he reminds readers that 'one of the African Christians' was 'that most godly and learned father Saint Augustine' (164), he also tells them that 'neither is there any region in all the Negroes land, which hath in it at this day any Christians at all'

(163). Whereas 'those which we before named white, or tawny Moors, are steadfast in friendship' (184), by contrast 'the Negroes lead a beastly kind of life, being utterly destitute of the use of reason, of the dextery of wit, and of all the arts. Yea they so behave themselves, as if they had continually lived in a forest among wild beasts. They have great swarms of harlots among them...'. Thus Africanus's text helps create a hierarchy within Africa that is colour-coded: if some Africans are as civil as Europeans, others are brutish and show no signs of being civilized.

Othello condenses this range of differences into a single individual, translating the tension between them into the social and psychic complexities of his being. The contradiction between dark skin and civility implied by Africanus's text resonates with Shakespeare's play, which also picks up on the religious tensions between Islam and Christianity as well as the European admiration for Moorish learning and valour. Thus *Othello* fuses various contemporary discourses of Moorish 'difference' which circulated in Shakespeare's times, reminding us that 'race' is not a homogeneous or clearly articulated category, but one that develops by drawing, often arbitrarily and contradictorily, upon various popular beliefs as well as more elite ideas, upon traditional notions as well as newer knowledges.

Shakespeare's play, I have suggested here, forges these beliefs about ethnic and religious difference, Africans, Moors, and Turks upon the anvil of gender difference. Yet here, as elsewhere, 'race' is also articulated with notions of 'class'. Iago's racial jealousy of the Moor is also a class envy of the servant who does not believe that his master has a right to be his master. Like Mosca in Jonson's play *Volpone*, Iago follows his master only waiting 'to serve my turn upon him' (*Othello*, 1.1.42). His master, moreover, was not born to his station; indeed being a Moor, he should not even have been able to acquire it. In Iago's eyes, Othello's colour should properly code him as Iago's inferior, it should undercut Othello's 'service' to the state as well as his 'royal' lineage. Iago operates by rhetorically asserting his bond with Othello as his servant even as he seeks to reverse their relationship by assuming control of Othello's actions. The 'temptation scene' (Act 3, scene 3) inverts the master–servant relationship as Iago assumes control of his master even as he states his own loyalty and subservience: 'I am your own for ever.'[20] Iago's vow echoes the marriage ceremony, and affirms a homosocial alliance which will wreak vengeance on the erring woman.[21]

Othello Today

At the beginning of this book I quoted Bloke Modisane, the South African writer who invokes *Othello* to question the racism of his own society. Whereas Paul Robeson and many others used their performances of *Othello* to focus on contemporary racism, the black British actor Hugh Quarshie questions the efficacy of such attempts:

if a black actor plays Othello does he not risk making racial stereotypes seem legitimate and even true? When a black actor plays a role written for a white actor in black make-up and for a predominantly white audience, does he not encourage the white way, or rather the wrong way, of looking at black men, namely that black men, or 'Moors', are over-emotional, excitable and unstable, thereby vindicating Iago's statement, 'These Moors are changeable in their wills'? Of all the parts in the canon, perhaps Othello is the one which should not be played by a black actor.

. . . Is there a problem with *Othello*? If there is, does the problem lie with me or with Shakespeare?

Interpretation inevitably brings revelation: when we interpret Shakespeare's plays, we reveal something about ourselves. But we may also legitimately consider what Shakespeare revealed about himself when he adapted and interpreted the original story from Cinthio... We credit him with sufficient imaginative power to believe that he could have fashioned a tale about a man coming to terms with the supposed betrayal and adultery of those closest to him without suggesting that a character's race determined his behaviour. Did he not do precisely this in *The Winter's Tale*?... The point is that Shakespeare, had he wanted could have done something similar: he could have told a tale of jealousy, betrayal and revenge without racial references. I suggest he chose the Cinthio story because he wanted to capitalize on the figure of the Moor. And I fear that figure still occupies the same space in the imagination of the modern theatre-goers as it does among Shakespeare's contemporaries.[22]

I have quoted Quarshie's remarks at some length because they remind us that our attempts to rescue Shakespeare's plays from the taint of racism may have something to do with the central place the Bard occupies in our own cultures and imaginations. It is not always possible to find in his plays the seeds of all that we regard as progressive and humane. Like Quarshie, Ben Okri also does not find it easy to read Othello as noble, heroic, glamorous or radical: 'When a Black man in the West is portrayed as noble it usually means that he is neutralised. When white people speak so highly of a Black man's nobility they are usually referring to his impotence. It is Othello's neutrality and social impotence that really frightens me.'[23] So while for some of us Shakespeare's hero may represent the playwright's effort to complicate the pictures of Moors that circulated in his culture, for others Othello remains trapped within a white view of Moors. *The Winter's Tale*, Quarshie reminds us, does not suggest that Leontes' jealousy has anything to do with his whiteness, but each of Othello's characteristics as a husband, as a man, as a soldier, is always traced to his racial identity. This itself may be the problem—whether we regard him as noble or debased, challenging or confirming stereotypes, Othello can only be read against a collective category called 'Moors'.

The Imperial Romance of Antony and Cleopatra

Written only a few years after *Othello*, *Antony and Cleopatra* (1606–7) looks at the intersection of racial difference, colonial expansion, and gender from a very different angle. In this play, Shakespeare reaches back to events which had occurred in the first century BC, and which had been repeatedly narrated by Roman and other storytellers from that time to his own. By taking as his central figure a foreign queen who was already a symbol of wanton sexuality and political seduction in European culture, Shakespeare comments on a long tradition of writing in which sexual passion expresses, but also ultimately sabotages, imperial ambition. Shakespeare harnesses a long history and wide geography to early modern English anxieties about women's power, foreigners, and empire. This chapter will highlight this layering of past and present, suggesting that racial ideologies fuse ideas received from different historical periods, and from both literate and popular cultures.

In an introduction to the play, Michael Neill contrasts 'Cleopatra's playful sense of herself as "with Phoebus's amorous pinches black"' (1.5.28) with 'Othello's anguished "Haply for I am black"' (3.3.267) in order to argue that 'the issue of racial difference' in this play is 'relatively insignificant'.[1] Cleopatra's attitude to her own skin colour might indicate that she does not think of it as a sign of inferiority, but it does not tell us that her colour is unimportant in Roman constructions of her as an Egyptian wanton, as the very antithesis of a chaste Roman wife. And Cleopatra is far from indifferent to what the

Romans think of her, although one of her strategies is to play up to, and exaggerate, their images of her. Even if she were indifferent, of course, that would not be evidence for a lack of racial tension in the play as a whole. Although skin colour is not the only marker of such tension, it is a good place to start examining different aspects of the history and myth of Cleopatra.

Although Cleopatra calls herself 'black', and Philo calls her 'tawny' (1.1.6), none of the repeated, hyperbolic, and contradictory descriptions of her in the play tells us much about her physically. She is the 'wrangling queen, | Whom everything becomes' (1.2.50–1); she is both 'Rare Egyptian' (2.2.224) and 'foul Egyptian' (4.13.10); she is a 'triple-turned whore' (4.13.13), 'a right gipsy' (4.13.28), and a 'vile lady' (4.15.22). Enobarbus' lyrical account of her on the barge describes the boat, the pavilion, the attendants, the perfume, the effect Cleopatra has on others—everything *but* her appearance: 'For her own person, | It beggared all description' (2.2.204–5). As with Othello, critics have sometimes suggested that Cleopatra is 'tawny' rather than black, and some Renaissance texts indeed registered the difference—Heylyn's *Microcosmus* says that Egyptians are 'not black, but tawny and brown'.[2] Shakespeare uses both terms in relation to Cleopatra, and many of his contemporaries used them interchangeably, referring to the 'tawny colour' of the 'Blackamoor'. Moreover, 'tawny' skin was not necessarily viewed as less offensive than black—Portia's suitor Morocco is called 'tawny' and yet she says he has the 'complexion of a devil'.[3]

We know that the historical Cleopatra, like the rest of the Ptolemaic dynasty that ruled Egypt, was of Greek descent, although the ethnicity of her grandmother is not known, and has led to some speculation about whether or not Cleopatra was of mixed race, or of dark colour. To complicate matters, ancient Greece was culturally, ethnically, and religiously diverse. Africa, especially Egypt, deeply influenced Greek society. This was acknowledged by the Roman writer Plutarch, whose *Lives of the Noble Grecians and Romans*, in Sir Thomas North's English translation, was a source for Shakespeare's *Antony and Cleopatra*. The Egyptians themselves were also a highly diverse people; Herodotus described them as having black skins and woolly hair, but both black and white persons are depicted on Egyptian vases and artifacts of the time. However, there *was* a distance between the Greek rulers of Egypt and its citizens—the rulers did not integrate with the common people or speak their language, although they identified strongly with the Egyptian gods Osiris and Isis.

In spite of this gap between Egyptian rulers and the populace, Roman historians identified Cleopatra as Egyptian; Cleopatra herself laid the ground for this by being the only Ptolemy to learn Egyptian, and to control popular unrest. Roman accounts of her as a luxurious wanton, given only to pleasure, deliberately ignore the fact that she was an astute political leader (retrospectively some Egyptian histories even cast her as a nationalist).[4] Like Ptolemaic queens before her, she encouraged identification of herself with Egyptian goddesses. Whereas they had used a single or a double 'uraeus' or cobra head as their symbol, Cleopatra used three cobras, perhaps in order to indicate her control over Upper Egypt, Lower Egypt as well as the additional territories which Antony gifted her. For the Romans, an identification between Cleopatra and Egypt was strategically necessary in order to highlight an absolute division between Rome and Egypt.

In Shakespeare's play too, Cleopatra is repeatedly identified with Egypt. She is called 'Egypt' by Antony (1.5.42; 3.11.51 and 56; 4.13.25; 4.16.19), by herself (1.3.41), and by her followers (4.16.74); she is 'Egypt's widow' (2.1.37), an 'Egyptian dish' (2.6.126), a 'serpent of Egypt' (2.7.26), a 'serpent of Old Nile' (1.5.25); her charms are, for Antony, 'these strong Egyptian fetters' (1.2.109) which he must break free from. In early modern Europe, Egyptians were widely grouped with other dark-skinned people of Africa and Asia as the descendants of Ham. Africanus repeats this belief that 'the Egyptians ... fetch their original from Mesraim the son of Chus, the son of Cham, the son of Noe [Noah]' (857). Thus, despite only two explicit references to it, Cleopatra's darkness is reinforced by suggestions that Cleopatra embodies Egypt.

But which Egypt does she embody? In early modern England, Egypt was known as a land of ancient religion, philosophy, and learning. There was an interest in Egyptian antiquity, and a flourishing trade in mummies, which were sold in vast quantities because they were used in various medicines—an English merchant, John Sanderson, recorded that over 600 pounds of mummy were exported at the end of the sixteenth century.[5] But Egypt was also increasingly identified as a Turkish dominion. It had been part of the Ottoman Empire since 1516; Leo Africanus, in his influential *History of Africa*, claimed that he had been in the city of Rasid when 'Selim the great Turke returned this way from Alexandria'.[6] According to Africanus, Egypt was now devoid of 'any true Egyptians' because the majority of the population, 'embracing the Mahumetan religion, have mingled themselves among the Arabians and Moores' (856). Henry Blount's *A Voyage into the Levant* confirmed that 'the light' of the ancient glory of Egypt was now 'almost quite extinct':

Now as for the Justice and Government, it is perfectly Turkish...only it exceeds all other parts of Turkey for rigor, and extortion; the reason is because the Turk well knows the Egyptian nature, above all other Nations, to be malicious, treacherous and effeminate, and therefore dangerous, not fit for Arms, or any other trust; nor capable of being ruled by a sweet hand.[7]

Blount sees Turkish cruelty as justified by the effeminate and malicious 'nature' of Egyptians, but Africanus suggests that they have become mixed with their Muslim masters. In similar vein, Cesare Vecellio's costume book depicted a lady of Cairo as heavily veiled in the Islamic fashion (Fig. 8).

The view that Egypt no longer contained pure Egyptians was reinforced by the confusion between Egyptians and the gypsies who had arrived in England from Scotland in 1500. Although historical research now traces their roots to Northern India, in early modern England gypsies were supposed to have originated in Egypt. Andrew Borde's *First Boke of the Introduction of Knowledge* (1542) connects their migration to England with the absence of 'real Egyptians' in Egypt itself: 'The people of the country be swart and doth go disguised in their apparel, contrary to other nations they be light fingered and...have little manner.... There be few or none of the Egyptians that doth dwell in Egypt for Egypt is repleted now with the infidel aliens.'[8] Thus, Egypt has been overtaken by 'infidel aliens' or Turks, just as England has been invaded with 'swart' Egyptians. In Shakespeare's time, then, 'Egypt' and 'Egyptian' did not indicate any one 'race' but conjured up images of various peoples, all of whom were regarded as dark-skinned and associated with 'Moors'. The effect of this confusion was to resurrect a central division between 'East' and 'West' which had been a feature of classical Roman and Greek

DONNA DEL CAIRO.

8. A heavily veiled lady of Cairo, from Cesare Vecellio, *Degli habiti antichi et moderne...*

literatures. Shakespeare's play refers to Cleopatra as both Egyptian and a gypsy, but it also identifies Egypt as the 'East'; more importantly, it plays upon a dichotomy between Rome and Egypt in which each is defined by its difference from the other.

History, Literature, and Empire

Imperial conquest is routinely demonstrated through the sexual possession of conquered women. Julius Caesar had an affair not just with

Cleopatra but with Eunoë, wife of King Bogudes the Moor. Alexander, whom Antony tried to emulate, married Roxana, daughter of a Persian king he conquered. But neither Alexander nor Caesar allowed their sexual liaisons to distract them from their imperial enterprise, and both returned home to conduct other missions of conquest. Antony's association with Cleopatra, by contrast, reversed the dynamics of sexual possession and signified not his victory but *hers*. Roman writers were alarmed that Antony 'forgot his nation, his name, the toga, the axes of power and degenerated wholly into the style of that monster [Cleopatra], in mind, in dress, in all manner of life'.[9] This is the fear we see animated in *Antony and Cleopatra*.

The historical Octavius (who went on to reign as the Emperor Augustus) represented his battle against Antony and Cleopatra as a patriotic war to save Rome. The opposition between a masculine Rome and a feminine 'East' animates Virgil's epic, *The Aeneid*, which was written to celebrate Augustus' reign. The epic narrates the story of another famous African queen, Dido, who was loved but abandoned by the Roman voyager Aeneas. Aeneas' shield is decorated with a depiction of the battle of Actium in which Antony and Cleopatra were defeated by Octavius. On one side stands lofty Augustus; on the other

> Antony,
> Egypt and all the East; Antony, victor
> Over all the lands of dawn and the Red Sea,
> Marshals the foes of Rome, himself a Roman,
> With—horror!—an Egyptian wife.[10]

Aeneas' resolve to leave Dido and return to his Roman duty implicitly criticizes Antony's capitulation to Cleopatra and celebrates the victory of Octavius/Augustus over the pair. Shakespeare's play returns to this victory, but infuses the event with loss and tragedy.

Edward Said's *Orientalism* suggests that such an opposition between 'the familiar (Europe, the West, "us") and the strange (the Orient, the East, "them")' has animated 'European imaginative geography' from Greek times till the present.[11] This suggestion has been criticized for being ahistorical—how could the same binary opposition be so important to different periods and cultures? Said, his critics say, is attributing a colonial vision of the East to pre-colonial times. As already discussed, the 'East' could hardly be regarded as Europe's 'other' during the Renaissance. Europeans desired to enter the powerful economic networks of the Mediterranean, Levant, North Africa, and Asia, feared the military might of the Turks, and were dazzled by the wealth and sophistication of many Eastern kingdoms. In fact recent scholars have gone so far as to suggest that Europe was really on the periphery of powerful economic networks whose centre was in the East, and that European global domination did not begin till the eighteenth century.[12] Moreover, there were interactions, cross-overs, and mixing between East and West which are overlooked by the suggestion of a binary opposition.

However, while we need to 'de-centre' Europe by historicizing its global dominance rather than assuming it was always in place, there are two central questions that we still have to contend with. One: if early modern Europe was peripheral to other powerful global economies, what explains the tilting of balance in its favour in the eighteenth century? A partial answer is that, though in the seventeenth century neither colonialism nor capitalism were fully formed, their wheels had been set in motion. Europeans may not have been able to colonize every part of the globe in the seventeenth century but certainly their position in the New World or in parts of the old (such as the Moluccas, or Goa) cannot be described as 'peripheral'. And two: even before colonialism, European (including English) writings do rehearse and repeat certain ideas about cultural and geographic difference. The Roman Empire may not have established Europe's global mastery, indeed the very idea of Europe did not exist at that time, but Roman imperial conquests did spawn negative images that were appropriated by later writers, especially because countries such as England looked towards Rome to establish their own genealogy as an imperial nation.

To acknowledge these repetitions is not necessarily to suggest a static unchanging discourse, or to misunderstand the actual power relations between 'East' and 'West' in different periods. Often, literary texts as well as historical documents reach back to previously established motifs in order to make them serve entirely new purposes, including that of establishing or asserting a superiority that does not exist. Shakespeare drew from Plutarch's tales about Cleopatra, but also infused them with other literary and cultural myths, as well as more contemporary materials, not because England was already an empire but because empire was one of the subjects of his play. Thus the older idea of a division between East and West, and specifically Egypt and Rome, energizes his play, although, as we will see, it is not as if England stands in for Rome in any straightforward way.

To some extent, all early modern European writings about non-European lands rehearse older accounts. For example, the Greek writer Herodotus had initiated the myth of *Egypt* as a land of inversion:

The Egyptians themselves in their manners and customs seem to have reversed the ordinary practices of mankind. For instance, women attend market and are employed in trade, while men stay as home and do the weaving ... men in Egypt carry loads on their heads, women on their shoulders; women pass water standing up, men sitting down.[13]

Johannes Boemus's *The Fardle of Facions* (1555) repeats this idea almost verbatim, but also infuses a specifically English imagery into it by commenting that Egyptian women 'revelled at the Tavern and kept lusty cheer: And the men sat at home spinning, and working of lace and such other things women are wont'.[14]

Picking up on this, Richard Knolles writes that Egyptian women always choose their own husbands. Similarly, Leo Africanus informs readers that the women of Cairo 'are so ambitious and proud, that all of them disdain either to spin or to play the cooks: wherefore their husbands are constrained to buy victuals ready dressed at the cooks' shops ...' (883). In repeating the idea of gender reversal, each of these reports also infuses it with contemporary references. Henry Blount even attributed it to Turkish occupation of Egypt, arguing that because Egyptians were a 'false and dangerous people', the Turkish Sultan Selim decided not to employ them as soldiers but use them to produce food for all his own people, 'whereby, without scandal, the Nation is made effeminate and disarmed' (54).

However, this is not to suggest that as time went on, there was a greater attempt to rationalize the idea of gender reversal. Often the opposite was true—as late as 1653, Bulwer's *Anthropometamorphoses* claimed that Egyptian men have breasts large enough to suckle their babies, while the women have 'small and manlike Breasts'.[15] Thus, what older texts regard as inversion of custom, Bulwer transforms into biological difference.

'Mankind' Women

Gender reversal is also central to the world of *Antony and Cleopatra*. Early in the play, Caesar comments that Antony's revelry in Egypt has effeminized him; Antony is now

> not more manlike
> Than Cleopatra, nor the queen of Ptolemy
> More womanly than he.
>
> (1.4.5–7)

Whereas in the writings mentioned earlier, gender reversal is contained within Egypt, in this play, it becomes an aspect of Egypt's relationship with Rome. By effeminizing Antony, Cleopatra threatens the hierarchy between imperial Rome and its dominion, Egypt:

> I laughed him out of patience, and that night
> I laughed him into patience, and next morn,
> Ere the ninth hour, I drunk him to his bed,
> Then put my tires and mantles on him whilst
> I wore his sword Phillipan.
>
> (2.5.19–23)

Such cross-dressing is not just bedroom play but manifests a larger reversal of gender roles. Cleopatra persuades Antony that they should fight the Romans by sea rather than land, a decision that is seen to unman not just Antony but all his Roman soldiers. Enobarbus pleads with Antony: 'Transform us not to women' (4.2.36) and Camidius laments: 'So our leader's led | And we are women's men' (3.7.68–9).

In Shakespeare's England too, debates about appropriate clothing were actually battles about status and identity. Authorities legislated the kind of clothing appropriate to people of different genders and classes. A proclamation of 1588 seeking to enforce 'the Statutes and Orders for Apparel' frowned against the 'inordinate excess in apparel' embraced by many of the queen's subjects, and claimed that such excess led to both a 'confusion of degrees of all estates' (i.e. a blurring of differences in social rank) as well as to the import of 'superfluity of foreign and unnecessary commodities'.[16] The proclamation suggests that to transgress the dress code is both to challenge existing social hierarchies and to endanger the 'natural merchandise of the realm' by relying on alien goods.

A popular pamphlet against female cross-dressing could spot transgressive women everywhere:

Since the days of Adam women were never so masculine: masculine in their genders and whole generations, from the mother to the youngest daughter; masculine in number, from one to multitudes; masculine in case, even from the head to the foot; masculine in mood, from bold speech to impudent action; and masculine in tense, for without redress they were, are, will be still most masculine, most mankind, most monstrous.[17]

Antony and Cleopatra speaks to these gender debates; for many, an Egypt where women are granted too much freedom and gender roles are reversed would have offered an uncomfortable parallel with contemporary England.

In Shakespeare's England, several people could spot parallels between Cleopatra's seduction of a great soldier, and Elizabeth's affair with her favourite, Essex, who ultimately betrayed her and was executed in 1601. Apart from the fact that both queens encouraged identifications of themselves with goddess figures (Elizabeth with the Virgin, Cleopatra with Isis), the crucial parallel between the English queen and the Egyptian legend was that as women, they both held onto political power against many odds. But, rather than simply evoking Elizabeth in any singular sense, Shakespeare's Cleopatra plays upon widespread cultural fears and fantasies about powerful, emasculating, and cross-dressing women, which are expressed in plays, pamphlets, sermons, laws, and conduct-books during both Elizabeth's rule and that of her successor, James I.

In Shakespearian plays, and in Shakespeare's day, intense liaisons with all women were regarded as potentially effeminizing. In *Antony and Cleopatra*, the danger posed by women is fused with that of foreign lands. Earlier we discussed how such fusion was also central to the myth of the Amazons, who were 'foreign' women evoked in order to contain female unruliness at home. The French essayist Montaigne writes:

For the queen of the Amazons replied to the Scythian who was inviting her to make love: '*The lame man does it best!*' In that feminine commonwealth, to escape the domination of the males, they crippled them from childhood—arms, legs, and other parts that gave men an advantage over them—*and made use of them only for the purpose for which we make of use of women over here.*[18]

Stories of Amazonian cruelty to men, Montaigne suggests, are projections of the real crippling of women in patriarchal Europe, a crippling that is necessary in order to produce compliant sexual partners. No wonder, then, that figures of Amazons abound in the debates about the proper place of women in England from the mid-sixteenth century onwards. John Knox's 'The First Blast of the Trumpet Against the Monstrous Regiment of Women' (1558), which was directed at Mary Tudor but appeared after Elizabeth had become queen, describes an England ruled by a queen as 'a world... transformed into Amazons'.[19]

Colour and Conversion

Antony and Cleopatra maps such concerns about powerful, foreign women onto an imperial theme. As it contemplated its place in the world, England looked back in conflicted ways to the legacy of imperial Rome. Rome was both a model for the English to emulate and a reminder that the English had themselves been colonized in the past. The literature and mythology of imperial Rome, and especially of Virgil's *Aeneid*, were freely appropriated by English monarchs, but often by editing the meanings of the original stories. For example, when Elizabeth was identified as Dido, the African queen's chastity and heroism in founding Carthage provided the basis of the comparison, which could only be sustained by disregarding her abandonment by Aeneas. James I also disregarded this feature of the original story in order to encourage identifications of himself with Aeneas.[20] James was also often identified as the new Augustus in official entertainments.

By the time Shakespeare wrote *Antony and Cleopatra*, the classical literary tradition was not the only one to represent an encounter between a feminine 'East' and a masculine 'West'. The biblical tale of the Queen of Sheba and the wise King Solomon also played upon this theme, and became a widespread cultural motif, as did stories of the Saracen princess who converts to Christianity and marries a European man. Leo Africanus had reported that Sheba was the queen of Ethiopia and had 'brought unto Salomon an hundred and twenty talents of gold, which amount to 720,000 golden ducats of Hungary, that is, seven tons of gold, and 20,000 Hungarian ducats besides...' (1032). Sheba gave all this wealth to Solomon after Solomon demonstrated his 'wisdom' to her; their contact resulted in a child called David who ensured that Ethiopia became a Christian land. The Sheba story sexualized the exchange of wealth and religion—an exchange that became a regular feature of the Renaissance stage. James encouraged identifications of himself with Solomon, and several English masques, pageants, and plays depicted foreign women gifting their wealth, beauty, and respect to Western monarchs, traders, and colonists. The homage-paying stranger or wild man of medieval court entertainments mutates into an 'Indian' king or queen in the London civic pageants, which were sponsored by various Livery Companies of London. Middleton's *The Triumphs of Honour and Virtue* (1622), for example, depicts 'a black personage representing India, called, for her odours and riches, the Queen of Merchandise'. She asks the viewer to observe her 'with an intellectual eye' and to see beyond her native blackness and to perceive her inner goodness, which has been made possible by her conversion to Christianity. 'Blest commerce' has brought English traders to her land, and made possible a wonderful trade between them—her wealth for their religion. All 'the riches and the sweetness of the East', she thinks, are fair exchange for the 'celestial knowledge' that is now hers (43–61).

The Sheba story was also collapsed into that of the 'black and beautiful' woman and her fair male lover in the biblical *Song of Songs*, also known as the *Song of Solomon*. As discussed in Chapter 2, medieval and Renaissance interpretations of the Song which suggested that the black woman was emblematic of the physical body in need of being blessed and whitened by the power of Christ incriminated the sexuality of real black women, as when the medieval divine Abelard compared such a body to 'the flesh of black women [which] is all the softer to touch though it is less attractive to look at'.[21] The beauty of black women increasingly began to represent the paradox of sexual desire, its power as well as its shame, and the connections between such desire and particular exotic, dangerous, or promising territories of the world.

The stories of Sheba and Solomon, and of the Shulamite in the *Song of Songs*, are collapsed into one another and also retold with renewed vigour during the Renaissance because these stories offer a framework which can enclose the attractions as well as the anxieties of colonial and mercantile contact. Kim Hall suggests that Solomon provided 'two models for relations between Western males and "Other" females'. In the first the 'white male refashion(s) and whiten(s) the dark foreign female into an object of transcendent wedded love' and in the second, 'Solomon (is) too much given to pleasures of the flesh, which are associated with the allures of a foreign female'.[22] I would like to suggest that both these models *simultaneously* shape the English theatricals which stage the encounter between foreign women and European men. The foreign woman is alluring, dangerous, and powerful, which makes her ultimate capitulation all the more meaningful. Thus the possibility of a European 'turning Turk' is averted by the conversion, assimilation (or in some cases death and destruction) of the alien woman.

This theme was revisited by many plays of the period. In Fletcher's *The Island Princess*, a Moluccan princess Quisara asks her Portuguese lover to convert to her religion. It ends with her own conversion to Christianity as the wife of another Portuguese suitor. In Philip Massinger's play *The Renegado*, Donusa, a niece of the Turkish Sultan, tries to convert her Italian lover Vitelli but finally converts to Christianity and escapes to Europe as Vitelli's wife. We find stories of Muslim and other foreign women's desire for white men not just in literary texts but also in some of the travelogues, although in the latter, such desire is often just speculation on the part of the European traveller and does not end in conversion or marriage. Stories about the Amazons also play upon a similar pattern, featuring the containment of an alien, seductive, and powerful woman, and in story after story, Amazonian queens are subdued and often married by Greek heroes like Theseus. The defeat and marriage of the Gothic empress Tamora in *Titus Andronicus*, we saw in Chapter 3, can also be situated within this scenario.

But there is a crucial difference between these plays and *Antony and Cleopatra*. These Amazonian figures and converted Muslim princesses are extremely fair, and their skin colour facilitates their assimilation into their new families. Dark-skinned women are allowed to pay homage to white men, but in English drama, they cannot be whitened, and cannot be invited to join the Christian family. The dark skin of Shakespeare's Cleopatra, the fact that she revels in it, and that Antony is ensnared by it, is thus especially striking. Earlier writers had visualized Cleopatra as black in order to indicate that inner virtue is more important than outer beauty, as in George Pettie's *A Petite Pallace*: 'Did not Antonius (that lusty gallant of this city) prefer Cleopatra that black Egyptian, for her incomparable courtesy, before all the blazing stars of this city? . . . Whereby you see that bounty before beauty is always to be preferred.'[23] Or else to suggest the blindness of love: Robert Greene's *Ciceronis Amor, or Tullie's Love* (1589) asks 'Is not Antony enamoured of the black Egyptian Cleopatra; Doth not Caesar envy in his love. . . . Affection is oft blind and deemeth not rightly, the blackest ebony is brighter than ivory.'[24] For the most part, however, in a culture that increasingly associated ideal femininity with whiteness, Cleopatra's fabled beauty was visualized as white, as in Chaucer's *The Legend of Good Women* which depicted her as 'fair as is the rose in May'.

In Shakespeare's play, Cleopatra's darkness is part of her intractability and her stubbornly Egyptian identity. The recurrent food imagery suggests her sexual availability and desirability: 'salt Cleopatra' is a tasty tidbit; she is Antony's 'Egyptian dish' (2.6.126), a 'morsel' that he found left on Caesar's plate (3.13.117). But Cleopatra does not remain a delicious treat for Roman men, making 'hungry where most she satisfies'; instead she threatens to devour them. She gleefully compares Antony to the fish she intends to catch:

> My bended hook shall pierce
> Their slimy jaws, and as I draw them up
> I'll think them every one an Antony,
> And say 'Ah ha, you're caught!'
>
> (2.5.12–15)

Such passages resonate with the Roman view of her as a predator, but they also remind us that Cleopatra is not Antony's Egyptian conquest. The role reversal complicates the pattern of representing the colonized land as a sexually available female.

Unlike the figures of Eastern royalty that were brought onto London streets in the mayoral shows, Cleopatra does not leave the shores of her native land and goes to great lengths to maintain her power within it. Like Quisara in *The Island Princess* and Donusia in *The Renegado*, Cleopatra is in love with a white man, but unlike them, she is sovereign as well as royal, and she does not surrender her sovereignty easily. She refuses to think of her relationship with Antony in matrimonial terms until he is dead, and is willing to negotiate with Caesar even while Antony is alive. After Antony's death, Cleopatra continues to resist being incorporated into Rome, although she now addresses Antony as 'husband'. Her suicide is double-edged: it outwits her would-be captors, but it also marks her adoption of 'the high Roman manner'—a trademark of Antony's culture. *Antony and Cleopatra* ends with the picture of the 'serpent of the old Nile' outwitting her adversaries by holding a snake to her breast, translating her defeat 'in this vile world' into 'immortal longings' (5.2.308, 276). Instead of a European converting an Eastern queen, in this play it is that queen who tempts him to 'flee himself'. Given the precariousness of the English toe-hold in Eastern lands at this period, we can appreciate the meaning of the recurrent image of a converted and compliant queen for audiences at home. A slippery Cleopatra, 'cunning beyond men's thought', takes on a special resonance here, playing upon the pattern, altering it.

Antony's predicament echoes Othello's—both are soldiers who have given themselves excessively to women who anchor them to a new but fraught cultural identity, but also lay them open to charges of unmanliness. Antony's passion makes him oscillate between his Roman martial self and a newly acquired 'Egyptian' identity, which appears incompatible with military valour. Cleopatra's followers are either women or eunuchs, and an 'unmanned' Antony joins their fawning assembly. Eunuchs were prominent symbols of the luxury and decadence of the Eastern empires, as well as of the potential of these empires to 'unman' Christians. Moreover, conversion to Islam entailed circumcision, which Christians viewed as a sort of castration. The theatre featured the threat of both to English identity—in *The Renegado*, the Turkish damsel Donusia is attended by Carazie, an English-born eunuch. In Heywood's *The Fair Maid of the West*, Gazet, a foolish English servant, hopes to gain wealth by converting to Islam but instead finds that he has been castrated. William Daborne's play *A Christian Turn'd Turk* depicted a conversion ceremony complete with circumcision; its hero Ward is circumcized and also 'unmanned' by his Turkish wife. *Antony and Cleopatra* pre-dates these other plays, but we can appreciate the contemporary significance of Antony's supposed loss of manhood in Egypt. The story of Antony and Cleopatra had always been a cautionary tale, a story that warned aspiring imperialists of the dangers of the East. We can understand why during Shakespeare's time, when the powerful markets of Asia and North Africa were both intensely desired and feared to lure Christians to Islam, this story acquired a new urgency.

Gypsy Lust

The dangers of Antony's conversion are announced in the opening lines of the play by his comrade Philo who tells the audience that Antony's 'captain's heart' seems to have 'become the bellows and the fan | To cool a gipsy's lust' (1.1.9–10). The slippage between 'Egyptian' and 'gypsy' reinforces the dangers of conversion in the play, and brings them closer home to England.[25] Samuel Daniel had previously associated Cleopatra with gypsies, as had Shakespeare himself in *Romeo and Juliet* where Mercutio says 'Laura to his lady was a kitchen wench ... Cleopatra a gypsy' (2.3.37–9). In early modern England, the confusion between Egyptians and gypsies was not limited to popular usage, but became part of English legal vocabulary. John Cowell's dictionary of legal terms, *The Interpreter* (1607) explained that English statutes defined Egyptians as

a counterfeit kind of rogues, that being English or Welch people, accompany themselves together, disguising themselves in strange robes, blacking their faces and bodies, and framing to themselves an unknown language, wander up and down, and under pretence of telling of fortunes, curing diseases, and such like, abuse the common people, by stealing all that is not too hot or heavy for their carriage ... These are very like to those, whom the Italian call Cingari ...[26]

Cowell suggests that English gypsies are fake rogues who only pretend to be gypsies by blackening their faces and appropriating a strange language. But 'real' gypsies were also regarded as inauthentic—John Florio's Italian–English dictionary defines the Cingari as 'the roguing Giptians that go filching about the countries' and Montaigne refers to gypsy women as 'Counterfeit Egyptian women who have shown up in our midst'.[27]

Gypsies were widely compared to Jews and Muslims, both of whom were also popularly associated with disguise, trickery, and conversion. Thomas Dekker writes:

They are a people more scattered than the Jews, and more hated. Beggarly in apparel, barbarous in condition, beastly in behavior and bloody if they meet advantage. A man that sees them would swear they had all the yellow jaundice, or that they were tawny Moors' bastards, for no Red-ochre man carries a face of a more filthy complexion. Yet are they not born so; neither has the sun burnt them so, but they are painted so.... If they be Egyptians, sure I am they never descended from the tribes of any of those people that came out of the land of Egypt.[28]

The defining feature of gypsies is their artifice; their darkness is not natural, and yet not less threatening for being artificial. Dekker pursues the idea of artifice further, comparing gypsies to 'Morris-dancers, with bells' and to actors ('like one that plays the Rogue on a Stage' (244)). It was often supposed that actors imitated 'Moorish' dances that Christians had become familiar with during the Crusades. The remark that gypsies look like 'tawny Moors' bastards' picks up on associations between Moors and gypsies that were rife since at least the mid-fifteenth century, when a Scottish laird who obliged the king by killing the captain of the gypsies adopted a Moor's head as his crest.[29] Early gypsies were also referred to as Saracens.

The confusion between gypsies and Egyptians only strengthened the association of each with Moors, since, as we've noted earlier, contemporary Egypt was understood to be overrun by the 'infidel' Moors and Turks. It also underlined their supposed propensity for artifice: in early modern sermons, travelogues, and histories, the prophet Mohammed is repeatedly called a 'juggler' and trickster. Thus Cleopatra's 'false soul', her theatricality, and her cross-dressing pick up a complex web of connections between gypsies, stage actors, Moors, as well as local tricksters. Antony claims that Cleopatra

Like a right gypsy hath at fast and loose
Beguiled me to the very heart of loss.

(4.12.28–9)

'Fast and loose' was one of the games with which gypsies were supposed to cheat the public. In his *Art of Juggling* (1612), Samuel Rid suggests that Egypt is the origin of such tricks:

Certain Egyptians banished (from) their country... arrived here in England, who being excellent in quaint tricks and devises, not known here at that time among us, were esteemed and had in admiration... insomuch that many of our English loiterers joined with them, and in time learned their craft and cozening. The speech which they used was the right Egyptian language, with whom our Englishmen conversing with, at last learned their language.[30]

Cleopatra as the 'enchanting queen' brings together magic associated with non-Western cultures, the sorcery associated with witches and enchantresses, domestic and alien, as well as the trickery associated with petty crime at home.

Royal acts of 1559 forbade the use of 'charms, sorcery, enchantments, invocations, circles, witchcrafts, soothsaying or any like crafts or imaginations invented by the Devil'; a statute of 1604 reinforced the prohibition.[31] Other legislation attempted to curb the tricks of gypsies and those who impersonated them. From 1530 onwards, the English authorities repeatedly banished gypsies from the realm and proclaimed harsh punishments for English people who associated with gypsies. In 1562, 'An Act for further punishment of vagabonds, calling themselves Egyptians' warned that anyone found

in any company or fellowship of vagabonds, commonly called or calling themselves Egyptians, or counterfeiting, transforming or disguising themselves by their apparel, speech or other behaviour, like unto such vagabonds... shall therefore suffer pains of death, loss of lands and goods, as in the cases of felony by the order of the common laws of this realm'.[32]

The legislation concerning gypsies reveals a fear of contamination that might pass from 'real' to 'false' gypsies and spread among the local populace; at the same time the laws suggest that all gypsies are 'counterfeit'. In April 1577, eight people were hanged for associating with gypsies; in May 1596, 106 men and women were condemned to death for 'having wandered in diverse parts of this realm in this country of York, some of them feigning themselves to have knowledge in palmistry, physiognomy, and other abused sciences, using certain disguised apparel and forged speech, contrary to diverse statutes and laws of this realm...'.[33] Eventually most of these people were deported back to their place of birth but nine of them were hanged because they were found to be 'strangers, aliens born in foreign parts across the seas, and none of the Queen Majesty natural born subjects'. English-born gypsies were treated differently to those considered 'foreign', and the laws sought to reinforce the distinction between the two, and to prevent any association between them.

'Egyptians' were regularly sentenced to death in England under these laws, but several contemporary commentators felt that legislation was not very effective, and Samuel Rid noted that even though Queen Elizabeth endeavoured

by all means possible to root out this pestiferous people, but nothing could be done, you see until this day: they wander up and down in the name of Egyptians, colouring their faces and fashioning their attire and garment like unto them, yet if you ask what they are, they dare no otherwise then say, they are Englishmen, and of such a shire, and so are forced to say contrary to that they pretend. (B2^{r-v})

Rid points out that gypsies can only make a living by pretending to be what they are not, and yet, given the laws of the land, they can never openly admit to the impersonation.

Gypsies were especially disliked by the authorities because they were not simply ungovernable individuals but formed tight communities with their own hierarchies and forms of governance; Rid mentions a Giles Hather and Kit Calot who 'style themselves the King and Queen of Egypt'. Analogously, Cleopatra is threatening to Rome because she is not just Antony's 'Egyptian wife' but a sovereign who resists Egypt's incorporation into the Roman Empire. Caesar is threatened because Antony gifts her entire kingdoms and territories which, in his view, belong to his empire. While English gypsies can hardly be read as embodying a similar threat of alternative governance and insurgency, stories of their theatrical and stubborn communities add another dimension to Shakespeare's depiction of the conflict between Rome and Egypt. Above all, the theme of Antony 'going native' or becoming an Egyptian by associating with Cleopatra and her train, brings together the fears of conversion generated by both the 'infidels' and imposters associated with Eastern empires, and the lowly gypsies. Gypsies, as well as Saracens and Muslims, are commonly spoken of in terms of a disease, a pestilence, an infection, that can threaten the health of the English body, and yet both are enormously seductive to Englishmen. The powerful Muslim empires hold out the promise of trade, luxury, and sensuality for the middle-class and noble adventurer, while the gypsies are similarly attractive to vagabonds and poor English wanderers.

Finally, it is the combination of uncontrollability and changeability in the gypsy lore that can be seen to inflect Shakespeare's picture of Cleopatra. Rid opens his book on juggling with the tale of the Moon asking her mother for a garment, 'comely and fit for her body: how can that be sweet daughter (quoth the mother) sith that your body never keeps itself at one stage, nor at one certain estate, but changeth every day in the month, nay every hour?' The gypsies were also called 'moon-men'; their slippery nature is also Cleopatra's. She is 'cunning past man's thought', a person of various moods and disguises. At the end of the play she claims to have become 'marble-constant' and renounces the moon as her governing deity: 'Now the fleeting moon | No planet is of mine' (5.2.236–7). However, even this gesture can be read as supreme theatricality, an attempt to outmanoeuvre Caesar and prevent him from displacing her from Egypt:

> Shall they hoist me up
> And show me to the shouting varletry
> Of censuring Rome? Rather a ditch in Egypt
> Be a gentle grave unto me . . .
>
> (5.2.54–7)

The Politics of Performance

Roman emperors had displayed their captives in the official triumphs, and during Shakespeare's time, European monarchs imitated this practice by recreating extravagant processions which showcased captured slaves, animals, and goods, and also displayed personifications of the territories they traded with or colonized. Given her own propensity for cross-dressing and for theatrical display, it is significant that Cleopatra is averse to the idea of being displayed by Caesar, and especially to the possibility that a Roman actor may impersonate her, or 'boy my greatness | I'th' posture of a whore' (5.2.216–17). The remark draws attention to the fact that throughout the play, the audience has been watching a white male actor, not an Egyptian woman or a gypsy, play the queen.

Do the racial and cultural metamorphoses that we see on the Renaissance stage, as well as in the plays, suggest a flexibility with regard to ideologies of skin colour and race in early modern culture? We need to be cautious while jumping to that conclusion. *Antony and Cleopatra*'s focus on performance and theatricality does not suggest that all identities are simply, or equivalently performative. Rather, it draws attention to the politics of performance—who is allowed to perform? Who is allowed to represent and appropriate others? Whose performance is effective? The answers, within the play, and in the culture at large, depend upon who has social and political power.[34] Whereas the poor vagabonds of England were persecuted for impersonating 'Egyptians', the upper classes flaunted such imper-sonations. In 1515 two ladies attended court with their heads rolled in gauze, tippers 'like the Egyptians, embroidered with gold' and their faces, necks, arms, and hands covered with black 'pleasance' so that they appeared to be 'negroes or black Mores'. In 1520 eight ladies appeared at a state banquet dressed also like Egyptians.[35] Among royalty and upper classes, the wearing of foreign clothes suggested their social and economic power rather than a collapse of their identity. Queen Elizabeth received Thomas Platter dressed in a white gown 'gold-embroidered, with a whole bird of Paradise for panache, set forward on her head studded with costly jewels'.[36] The rare bird was found only in the East, and England had recently staked its claim in the Moluccas. All over Europe, the upper classes borrowed Asian fabrics, designs, and patterns, and court fashions reflected the contact between Europe and these other worlds. To mention one example here, the exposing of breasts among European court ladies may have been inspired by the transparent smocks ('bajus') that were worn in Goa by wives and mistresses of the Portuguese.[37]

Court entertainments went a step further—nobility and royalty impersonated gypsies, the Irish, Asians, and Africans, but the disguises were often dismantled at the end. Jonson's masque *The Gypsies Metamorphosed* in which several noblemen shed their disguises as gypsies was a favourite with King James. We have already mentioned *The Masque of Blackness* and *The Masque of Beauty* in which Queen Anne and her ladies blacked up as 'Mores' but were magically transformed to whiteness at the end. Such impersonations and cross-dressing, by controlling the terms and direction in which identities were 'exchanged', were reassuring in the context of pervasive fears that Englishmen would go 'native' or lose their identities overseas. *The Masque of Gypsies* was published in 1621; the very next year, Lord Keeper Williams asked the Justices of Berkshire to enforce the laws against the 'whole troupe of rogues, beggars, Egyptians and idle persons' in that county.[38] An ideology which does not pathologize racial difference may be less pernicious than one which does, but that does not necessarily make the former either benign or ideologically flexible. The supposed fluidity of dark-skin colour that we see in the court masques works to reinforce the ultimate power of whiteness over it. Moreover, these theatrical scenarios of assimilation do not reflect an actual openness in the culture at large. Official legislation throwing out Jews, gypsies, and blacks reflects a fear of contamination; at a more popular level too there is a distrust of foreigners and outsiders. The contemporary diatribes against cross-dressing, against actors, as well as against Englishmen 'turning Turk', show that at least one section of the population feared, rather than embraced or celebrated, fluidity.

In *Antony and Cleopatra*, Antony's fatal attraction to Cleopatra speaks to contemporary English fears about the erosion of racial identity and masculinity. But the play offers no reassuring scenario of a foreign queen's assimilation. Cleopatra's love for Antony does not mean that she will submit to Rome. She plays with different personas to control Antony as well as to negotiate with Casear; in the end, she becomes *both* the goddess Isis, with an asp at her breast, as well as Antony's Roman wife. These images are contradictory, but Cleopatra inhabits them both. Cleopatra's 'Egyptian' self is constructed both by her and by the Romans; it is an essential aspect of the political struggle between the imperial power and its would-be colony. Cleopatra plays the Egyptian flamboyantly, thus appropriating, and flaunting the difference that Rome assigns to her. She knows that performance is a sign of power—she must impersonate whom she wants but no one else must be allowed to represent her. Once she has lost political power, and knows she will no longer be able to control the terms of the performance, she stages her suicide, the last performance she can script. Similarly, the extent to which Antony 'goes native' or remains a 'Roman' is determined by his need to gain a foothold in Egypt, a place from which he can assert himself against Caesar. His oscillations are controlled by Cleopatra on the one hand, and Caesar on the other because his position in Egypt depends upon the former, and in Rome upon the latter.

Thus the play suggests that to be an Egyptian or a Roman is to play certain roles which are defined by their difference from one another. But this does not mean that these roles can just be chosen at will, put on and discarded when one likes. Rather, they are shaped by long histories as well as political and cultural antagonisms. Individuals give these roles their particular meanings and force, but do not entirely control them. By showing us how identities which we call ethnic, or cultural or racial are fluid and yet not, for that reason, easy to manipulate, *Antony and Cleopatra* captures the contradiction that lies at the heart of race.

Religion, Money, and Race
in The Merchant of Venice

Salman Rushdie's *The Moor's Last Sigh* is the story of the marriage between a Christian girl and a Jewish man of Cochin, India, and of their child, who is called the 'Moor' both because his skin is dark, and because his mother lovingly nicknames him 'mór' ('peacock' in Hindi). In telling his saga about strife and love in a multi-religious, multiracial land, Rushdie harks back to the various migrations of Muslims, Christians, and Jews into India from the West. The Portuguese Christians came in search of trade, the Jews much earlier in order to escape persecution in Spain and Portugal, and the Muslims for both those reasons. All of them were to eventually fight over control of the pepper trade, but also to intermarry and consort with one another, and indeed with other communities in India. In narrating their tale, Rushdie goes back to *The Merchant of Venice* (1596–7) and *Othello*, both of which speak of similar tensions and loves, and to the period in history they dramatize, when outward journeying catalysed the internal tensions of Europe.

Rushdie contrasts his Aurora, who defies her family to marry a Jew, with Portia, who can only bring herself to address Shylock twice by his name, and who will not flout her father's will that she marry the man who chooses between three caskets of gold, silver, and lead to find the one that contains her picture. Portia, 'the very archetype of justice', Rushdie notes, is rather pleased when the 'tawny' Prince of Morocco fails to choose the right casket:

A gentle riddance. Draw the curtains, go.
Let all of his complexion choose me so.

(2.7.78–9)

Rushdie comments that Portia is 'No lover of Moors...I adduce all
this evidence to show why, when I say our tale's Aurora was no Portia,
I do not mean it wholly as a criticism'.[1] Although Christian, his
Aurora is not European; she is 'near the height of her very Indian
beauty'. In Shakespeare's play Bassanio compares such beauty to a
'dangerous sea' as he explains that he chose the right casket by being
able to distinguish between appearance and reality:

Ornament is but the guilèd shore
To a most dangerous sea, the beauteous scarf
Veiling an Indian beauty; in a word,
The seeming truth which cunning times put on
To entrap the wisest.

(3.2.97–101)

The phrase 'Indian beauty' is oxymoronic, since 'Indian' indicates
a dark skin, which Portia has already called repulsive. The lady
(assuming it is a lady because the gender of the 'beauty' is not spelt
out) is like 'cunning times', unattractive but made alluring by her
beauteous scarf. If the beholder is fooled and fails to recognize her
danger, the result will be miscegenation, a subject that haunts the
caskets episode and the play as a whole. Rushdie concludes that the
terms on which both justice and romance are developed in *The
Merchant of Venice* demand that Moors, Indians, and Jews be 'waved
away' (115).

A large and international group of suitors establishes the worth of
Portia's 'sunny locks', but only an insider can win Portia, because only
an insider can recognize the difference between inner and outer selves,
appearance and reality. Ironically, Portia herself refuses to make this
distinction in the case of Morocco, admitting that even if he were a
saint, she would not be able to overlook his blackness: 'If he have the
condition of a saint and the complexion of a devil, I had rather he
should shrive me than wive me' (1.2.126–8). Portia informs Morocco
that he must

swear before you chose, if you chose wrong
Never to speak to lady afterward
In way of marriage.

(2.1.40–2)

Some critics suggest that this injunction is reserved for Morocco alone, failing to notice that the Prince of Aragon also promises 'never... | To woo a maid in way of marriage' should he fail to win Portia (2.9.12–13). Portia confirms that every suitor of hers must swear to abide by this rule. Thus, although she expresses her dislike for Morocco in stronger and undoubtedly more racialized terms, both he and the Spaniard are cast as outsiders to a culture that encompasses both Venice and Belmont. Sexual reproduction must be tightly controlled, and those who foolishly imagine they can cross cultural boundaries must not be allowed to reproduce at all.

In England, Spain was commonly regarded as the site of rampant miscegenation: in Edmund Spenser's *A View of the Present State of Ireland*, Irenius laments that although the Moors were 'beaten out by Ferdinand of Aragon and Isabella his wife, yet they were not so cleansed but that, through the marriages which they had made and mixture with the people of the land during their long continuance there, they had left no pure drop of Spanish blood... So that, of all the nations under heaven, I suppose the Spaniard is the most mingled and most uncertain.'[2] Although the play builds upon many features of contemporary Italy, such as its cosmopolitanism, its international trade, and the wealth of its upper classes, it uses them, as does *Othello*, to address specifically English anxieties about commerce, race, and sexuality.

The play makes clear the overlaps as well as crucial differences between sexual and economic traffic. Strangers, Antonio says, have great 'commodity' in Venice because 'the trade and profit of the city | Consisteth of all nations' (3.3.27, 30–1). In such a society, where the reproduction of wealth depends upon international traffic, the dangers of miscegenation run high. Precisely because trade with Morocco was highly desired during this period, the desires of its prince for a white Christian woman must be strictly regulated. That is partly why Morocco is cast, not as a trader, but as a Muslim warrior, brandishing a 'scimitar', a curved sword used by Turks and Persians. Such a figure is reminiscent of the Crusades, although he makes it clear that he has used his sword to vanquish other Muslim princes rather than Christians.

But while some border crossings are taboo, others are encouraged. Portia, the rich Christian heiress, is like the 'golden fleece' who must be protected from the 'many Jasons [who] come in pursuit of her' (1.1.172), but Jessica, the wealthy Jew's daughter, can be allowed into the Christian family, especially because she promises to 'gild myself | With some more ducats' (2.6.49–50). Her passage is not necessarily smooth, as we learn from the exchange between Launcelot Gobbo and Jessica later in the play. Launcelot assures Jessica that despite her marriage, she is 'damned' by her Jewish lineage. When she protests that she will be 'saved by my husband', who 'hath made me a Christian', Launcelot grumbles that such conversions will only result in hardships for other Christians because by increasing the Christian, pork-eating population, they will 'raise the price of hogs' (3.5.17–22). Lorenzo puts an end to these complaints by evoking the spectre of a far more untenable crossing of racial lines—the 'getting up' of a 'Negro's belly' by Launcelot himself. Such a liaison, Lorenzo reminds Launcelot, can be even less justified to the 'commonwealth'; it cannot be sanctified by matrimony, because the lady is black. The 'Moor' in question is dismissed by Launcelot: 'if she be less than an honest woman, she is indeed more than I took her for' (3.5.39–40). In this context, it is worth recalling that one of the grounds on which Elizabeth I evicted 'Negars and Blackamoors' from England in 1596 was 'the annoyance of her own liege people that want the relief which those people consume'.[3] Earlier, Launcelot had claimed that he was being 'famished' in Shylock's service. Now, it is revealed that he has produced another non-Christian mouth to feed, a crime worse than Lorenzo's. Lars Engle points out that Launcelot's Moor, like so many in Christian households of the time, may have been a slave; the possibility that Portia is a slave owner prepares the audience for the next scene in which no one rebuts Shylock's accusation that the Christians have 'many a purchased slave | Which ... You use in abject and in slavish parts | Because you bought them' (4.1.89–92).[4] The links between conversion and inflation in this scene underline the play's interest in interweaving sexual and racial exchanges with economic ones.

Shylock's early exchange with Antonio about usury anticipates this interest. Shylock justifies taking interest by citing the biblical tale of how Jacob manipulated the reproduction of Laban's sheep. Since the agreement between Laban and Jacob was that the latter would get all the 'streaked and pied' offspring of the sheep he tended, Jacob waved striped bark in front of the sheep as they were doing 'the work of generation'. This ensured that they produced 'parti-coloured lambs', a manipulation that, in Shylock's view, represented 'thrift', for which Jacob was blest (1.3.84–8). This story from the Bible was widely cited by medical and other writers in the early modern period to affirm that 'what is strongly conceived in the mind, imprints the force into the infant conceived in the wombe', as the French surgeon Ambroise Paré wrote in his popular *Of Monsters and Prodigies*.[5] Paré uses the story to account for the birth of 'monsters', which include children who are a different colour from their parents (Fig. 9). He says that Hippocrates also employed it to free 'a certain noble woman from suspicion of adultery, who being white her self, and her husband also white, brought forth a child as black as an Æthiopian, because in copulation she strongly and continually had in her mind the picture of the Æthiope' (978). Here the woman does not actually have sex with a black man, but the result is the same—a black child born to a white woman, which George Best had cited as proof that blackness was a kind of 'inflection' that passed on in the blood.[6] Thomas Lupton's *A Thousand Notable Things of Sundrie Sorts* (1579), a book which was republished twice before *The Merchant* was written, shifts the same story to Spain which was widely associated with inter-religious sex. In its version, a 'noble matron' of Spain produced a black child, and was accused of having 'lain with some one of the slaves of the Saracens'. A wise man inspected her bedchamber which had the picture of an Ethiopian, and pronounced, citing the story of Laban's sheep, that although the woman was innocent, the 'great Ethiopian was the father of the child'.[7] Thus Shylock's defence of usury and economic growth evokes a scenario that was widely connected to miscegenation.

Antonio challenges Shylock's comparison between economic and sexual reproduction, claiming that the sheep were naturally produced ('fashioned by the hand of heaven'), and implying that, in contrast, Shylock's money-making is unnatural:

9. A black child born to white parents, shown alongside a hairy woman in Ambroise Paré's *Workes.*

> The devil can cite Scripture for his purpose.
> An evil soul producing holy witness
> Is like a villain with a smiling cheek,
> A goodly apple rotten at the heart.
> O, what a goodly outside falsehood hath!
>
> (1.3.97–101)

If Morocco has the devil's appearance, Shylock has his cunning. Antonio casts him as a white devil whose outward appearance belies his inner reality, and who can distort the scriptures to support his point of view. Such comparisons between Jews and the devil were commonplace in medieval writings but, according to James Shapiro's thickly documented study of Jews in early modern England, they had 'virtually disappeared' in sixteenth-century England. Shapiro argues that this period was as a 'crucial conduit' between the ages, a time when some medieval notions about Jews were discarded, and others appropriated to be recast as 'medically or scientifically sound evidence'.[8] We have traced similar processes in relation to ideologies about blacks, Muslims, and 'Egyptians'. Antonio resurrects the stereotype of the devilish Jew in order to articulate contemporary anxieties about Jews.

The Merchant of Venice is the only play in which Shakespeare pays extended attention to the relationship between commerce and race. The radical economic transformations of the early modern period had two apparently contradictory effects—on the one hand they encouraged the assumption that money was colour-blind and that wealth would override other social differences. On the other hand, racial differences became more, not less, pronounced during this period. Through the figures of various 'strangers' to Venice, but most especially through Shylock and Jessica, Shakespeare's play captures these contradictions. Jews were both insiders and outsiders, with deep roots in Europe, but also with long histories of persecution and migration. They were often indistinguishable, both physically and in terms of their activities, from the local populations, and yet they were marked as different, ideologically and often literally through clothing and confinement in ghettos. That difference was elusive, hard to define, and yet culturally central, and this is the dynamic encoded in *The Merchant of Venice*.

Shylock's Difference

Antonio suggests that Venetian law is blind to cultural, ethnic, and religious distinctions:

> For the commodity that strangers have
> With us in Venice, if it be denied,
> Will much impeach the justice of the state . . .

(3.3.27–9)

Contemporary travelogues were awed by the sheer number of 'strangers' in Italy: 'I think verily that in one region of the world again are not half so many strangers as in Italy,' wrote one visitor in 1549.[9] Jews made up large numbers of these 'strangers', although they were not visitors but residents. Venice was among the most tolerant of Italian states because most dependant upon Jewish participation in its economy, but even in Venice, Jews were required to wear a cap distinguishing them from others, to pay higher taxes, and be confined to the ghetto.[10] Shylock does not live in a ghetto, and he wears no special badge of identification, although he does mention his Jewish 'gaberdine', or long coat (for which critics have not been able to identify a historical source). Rather than remaining faithful to reports about Venetian Jews, Shakespeare plays upon three important elements which were repeatedly mentioned by contemporary writings— the economic importance of Jews, the tension between them and the Christians, and the supposed impartiality of the Venetian state towards the different communities in the city. David C. McPherson has suggested that the last feature was an important aspect of the 'Myth of Venice', or an idealized picture of Venice that was often used by English writers to reflect upon their own government and society. But in this play, as in *Othello*, the fabled cosmopolitanism and justice of Venice are exposed as flawed. By the end of the play, the Venetian legal system has revealed the double standard at its core:

> It is enacted in the laws of Venice,
> If it be proved against an alien
> That by direct or indirect attempts
> He seek the life of any citizen,
> The party 'gainst the which he doth contrive
> Shall seize one half his goods; the other half
> Comes to the privy coffer of the state ...

$$(4.1.345-51)$$

Although Venice is dependent upon Jews, it has special legal provisions to deal with 'aliens' who have instigated violence against 'citizens'. By the end of the play, Jews are cast as aliens to Venice, although earlier they have been acknowledged as part of its wealth-generating citizenry.

In 1595, about a year before *The Merchant* was staged, over a thousand artisans and apprentices in London had rioted violently against foreigners. James Shapiro points out that the play rewrites the dynamics of this hatred by casting a Jew as the instigator of the violence: 'The hostility is reimagined as originating with the aliens and directed against the citizenry and is enacted in a way that does not contradict the more tolerant laws governing the freedom of the city that guarantees equality before the law to strangers' (189). Thus the play is shaped not just by reports of Jewish life in Venice, but also by a specific English situation. In 1594, London had also been rocked by the controversy surrounding the trial of Roderigo Lopez, a Portuguese Jewish convert who was Queen Elizabeth's physician and was accused of poisoning her. Although the part played by his Jewishness in the trial remains open to debate, Lopez's execution ensured the success of a rerun of Christopher Marlowe's play, *The Jew of Malta*, which had played to packed houses in the 1590s. As discussed earlier, England had been one of the first countries to expel Jews in 1290, and they were not officially allowed back until 1656. For this reason scholars have often assumed that there were not enough Jews in Shakespeare's England for there to have been a 'Jewish Question' for him and his contemporaries.[11] It is true that Jewish characters such as Shylock and Barabas embody negative traits shared by the society at large, such as the greed for money, and therefore they can be seen as shorthand for a critique of such evil. But we still need to ask why Jews are used as shorthand, and why it is that the plays simultaneously question the difference between them and the Christians around them and focus relentlessly on their Jewishness.

Recent historians and critics have persuasively argued that, as with the black presence in England, numbers cannot be the only index to the cultural centrality of Jews and to the anxieties aroused by them. They have shown that in Shakespeare's time, there existed a small but significant Jewish community in England, comprised of physicians, teachers, and merchants, most of whom had begun to arrive there after the expulsions of Jews in Portugal and Spain. Although these Jews could not practice their faith openly (indeed some would argue that it was *because* they could not), their presence complicated the anti-Semitic ideologies that had percolated down from earlier times. Apart from England, Spain, and Portugal, Jews had, at different points of time, been expelled and readmitted, and sometimes expelled again, from various other places in Europe including Naples, Genoa, and Florence. Partly as a result, European Jews travelled to far-flung places; Samuel Purchas commented that 'dispersions of the Jewish nations' extended far beyond Europe to Africa, and especially Asia.[12]

At one time over 250,000 Jews lived in the Ottoman Empire, where many of them not only became successful traders but were appointed to high political positions.[13] In Marlowe's *The Jew of Malta*, Barabas the Jew is appointed governor of Malta by the Turks. The French traveller Nicholas de Nicholay, whose account of Turkey was translated into English in 1585, wrote that in Constantinople Jews indulged in trade as well as usury, and concluded that 'at this present day, they have in their hands the most and greatest of traffic of merchandize and ready money that is in all Levant'.[14] Nicholay reproduced the figure of a 'merchant Jew' of the region (Fig. 10); such traders offered stiff competition to English merchants seeking to establish a foothold in the lucrative trade in this region, and some English merchants believed that they could achieve their aims only by converting Jewish merchants to Christianity. Many of the Jews of Venice were in fact Sephardic merchants from Ottoman Turkey.

The racial, economic, and sexual tensions of *The Merchant* are woven from aspects of the Jewish presence in all these places, both as it was directly experienced by English people, and as it circulated through travel, religious, and other writings. Scholars have identified a wide range of physical and moral traits that were attributed to Jews during the medieval and early modern periods in Europe. Jews were supposed to stink (and become perfumed if they converted to Christianity), have large hooked noses, drink Christian blood, and Jewish men were said to menstruate and be capable of breast-feeding. They were accused of ritually murdering children, of poisoning Christians (perhaps because they were often renowned as physicians), of forcibly circumcizing Christian men, of indulging in cannibalism, of desecrating the eucharistic host, and, of course, exploiting Christians economically through usury. These prejudices fluctuated in different

10. A Merchant Jew from Nicholas de Nicholay, *The Navigations, Peregrinations and Voyages Made into Turkey.*

places and times, the hooked noses disappearing at one time, and the associations with usury intensifying at another. Barabas in *The Jew of Malta* embodies many of these attributes, and, like Aaron in *Titus Andronicus*, he revels in them:

> I walk abroad o' night
> And kill sick people groaning under walls:
> Sometimes I go about and poison wells
>
> .   .   .   .   .
>
> Being young, I studied physic, and began
> To practice first upon the Italian;
> There I enriched the priests with burials,
> And always kept the sextons' arms in use
> With digging graves and ringing dead men's knells:
> And after that was I an engineer,
> And in the wars 'twixt France and Germany,
> Under pretence of helping Charles the Fifth,
> Slew friend and enemy with my stratagems.
> Then after that was I an usurer,
> And with extorting, cozening, forfeiting,
> And tricks belonging to the brokery,
> I filled the jails with bankrupts in a year,
> And with young orphans planted hospitals,
> And every moon made some or other mad,
> And now and then one hang himself for grief
>
> .   .   .   .   .
>
> But mark how I am blest for plaguing them;
> I have as much coin as will buy the town.[15]

Barabas's equally villainous slave Ithamore is a Moor, and they proclaim their anti-Christian alliance: 'we are villains both: | Both circumcised, we hate Christians both' (2.3.216–17).

This alliance was widely suggested in contemporary writings. The medieval *The Play of the Sacrament* narrates the story of the conversion to Christianity of a Jonathas, 'chief merchant of the Jews'.[16] Curiously, 'almighty Mahomet' is Jonathas's 'glorious God' whose 'laws tenderly I have to fulfil' (ll. 149–50, 154). John Foxe wrote that 'it is supposed of some, this filthy Alchoran, not to be set out in the days of Mahumet, but that certain Jews had some handling also in this matter, and put it out after his death'.[17] Various writers repeated the idea that the prophet was born of a mixed marriage, and that his mother was 'a Jew blinded with superstition'.[18] The association between Jews and Muslims was underlined by their interlocking histories in Spain. The position of the two communities was far from identical there, but their expulsions and forced conversions had provoked analogous anxieties about the nature of religious and racial identity. Some of those associations spilled over into England, which had its own worries about English conversions to Islam as well as Jewish conversions to Christianity.

John Florio's Italian–English dictionary defined 'Marano' as 'a Jew, an Infidel, a renegado, a nickname for a Spaniard'.[19] Here, Florio describes converted Jews by evoking both Turks, and Europeans who had converted to Islam. A seventeenth-century English pamphlet literally conflated Moors and Jews, suggesting that 'when Ferdinand drove the Jews out of Spain, a world of them came into Africa, being born Moors, though of religion Jews'.[20] Nicholas de Nicholay indicated a more recent and pragmatic alliance by noting that 'the Maranes of late banished out of Spain and Portgual' had 'to the great detriment and damage of Christianity' taught the Turks 'diverse inventions, crafts and engines of war' but also made available to them 'books in diverse languages' (130–1). And a Spanish visitor wrote that the Jews had 'taught our enemies most of what they know of the villainies of war'.[21] Thus, both in the context of the trade networks which the Europeans desperately wanted to enter, and in the context of their own enmity with the Turks, an alliance between Jews and Muslims would have been worrying.

It is significant, then, that travelogues of the period also routinely suggest a tension between Muslims and Jews. William Biddulph writes that the Jews of Constantinople have to wear blue hats as marks of identification and 'are of more vile account in the sight of the Turks than Christians; insomuch that if a Jew would turn Turk, he must first turn Christian before they will admit him to be a Turk'.[22] The idea that Jews must first convert to Christianity before they can be admitted to Islam is repeated by other writers. Nicholas de Nicholay adds that Turks hold Jews in 'disdain and hatred' and will not eat with them, or 'marry any of their wives and daughters, notwithstanding that oftentimes they do marry with Christians' (131). Leo Africanus had found that 'Jews are had in great contempt by all men' in Fez, where they are made to pay a high tax, are forbidden to wear any shoes, and made to wear a black turban as a mark of identification.[23] The preacher Edward Terry claimed that Jews were hated in India. The most revealing comments are made by William Davies, who laments the fact that 'a Jew is respected more in Christendom, than with the Turks' for Turks make Jews wear a 'black cap ... to show the world that he is a Jew and a slave to the world' and say that 'if a Jew had put Mahomet to death, nay, but touched the hem of his garment violently, they would not have left one of the race alive ... but in Christendom they are suffered to build synagogues, and to use their religion publicly'. But he concludes by beseeching God 'that this our land of England may never be defiled, whether by a Pope, Turk or Jew'.[24]

Thus Turkish hatred for Jews becomes an argument for increased Christian intolerance against them. An emphasis on an antipathy between Muslims and Jews, I suggest, was partly a response to the acute anxieties generated by their widely feared alliance. According to some analysts, comparison of Jews and Muslims was a major factor in fuelling anti-Semitism. Europe perceived itself to be besieged by militant Islam, and the Jew was regarded as an 'Islamic fifth columnist in Christian territory'.[25] This hypothesis certainly reverberates with *The Merchant of Venice* where the threat posed by 'Moors' (both tawny and black, male and female, living in Venice and outside it) is both contrasted to and mirrored by the threat posed by the Jews who live within Venice.

In literary, theological, and other writings, Jews were also associated with blackness, an association that was analogous to, and later interconnected with, the conflation of Islam and blackness. In *Titus Andronicus*, the black villain Aaron is given a Jewish name. In *The Merchant of Venice*, Jessica reinforces this association by naming 'Cush' or Chus, widely believed to have been the progenitor of all blacks, as one of Shylock's countrymen' (3.2.283). The idea of the moral and often literal blackness of Jews and of Judaism had as long a tradition as that of the blackness of Islam; it was reinforced as racism intensified, so that in nineteenth-century Germany, the Jew could be labelled the 'white Negro'.[26] Not surprisingly, analogies between Jews and blacks surfaced as the blood laws were codified in Spain; in a passage we have already considered, a Spanish writer compared the 'blackness' of 'Negroes' to 'the ingratitude of Jews' by suggesting that both these qualities are inherent and persist, even if Jews convert and black people 'unite' with white women.[27] While the specificity of racism against Jews, Moors, and blacks should not be blurred by these overlaps, they remind us that analogies between different marginalized groups, as the ones we noted earlier between women and blacks, play a crucial role in the construction and circulation of racist ideologies.

In *The Merchant of Venice*, the Christians refer to Shylock as 'devil' (1.3.96; 2.2.19), or 'the very devil incarnation' (2.2.25), 'old carrion' (3.1.33), and most often merely 'Jew', rarely calling him by his name. Shylock himself says that they 'call me misbeliever, cut-throat, dog, | And spit upon my Jewish gaberdine' (1.3.110–11); Antonio merely confirms that 'I am as like to call you so again' (1.3.128). The play vividly evokes the difference perceived by both Jews and Christians between their two communities: Shylock says he bears 'an ancient grudge' against Antonio because the latter is a Christian who 'hates our sacred nation' and 'my tribe' (1.3.45, 46, 49). He draws a line between economic and other kinds of interactions: 'I will buy with you, sell with you, walk with you, and so following, but I will not eat with you, drink with you, nor pray with you' (1.3.33–5). Although no critic can ignore this antipathy in the play, scholars have been divided over what it means. One strand of scholarship has insisted that anti-Jewish sentiment in the medieval and early modern periods should be defined as theologically driven rather than racial in nature.[28] But as recent work on Jews in Europe suggests, this is an unhelpful formulation, since religion and race are so tightly woven together. What is more, as Jerome Friedman demonstrates, racist views about Jews hardened as a result of the anxieties regarding religious conversion in Iberia.[29] In medieval Europe, he says, hatred of the Jews focused on their supposed unwillingness to convert and assimilate into Christian society; in early modern Europe on the other hand, the tensions arose precisely from the fact that thousands of Jews *did* convert, forcibly or otherwise. Although many converts quietly assimilated, others were regarded as retaining their Jewishness, either by covert practices or by their very nature. The process of trying to pinpoint the difference between these converts and the Old Christians led to 'a growing identification of Jewishness as biological fate and infection, both physiologically and spiritually, to be cut out of society rather than incorporated into it' (27).

In England, similar tensions were central to the racialization of Jews; one critic argues that as early as the thirteenth century in England, 'there was an irreducible element to Jewish identity in the eyes of Christians, which no amount of baptismal water could entirely eradicate'.[30] By Shakespeare's time, Jewish conversion posed a major dilemma; on the one hand, widespread conversion of Jews to Christianity was widely regarded as a prerequisite to the Second Coming of Christ, and therefore to be welcomed. On the other, conversions eroded the idea of a distinct Christian identity, and generated anxiety as well as hatred towards the convert. Again, what heightened these concerns was the assumption that many Jews would never genuinely convert and would retain, indeed, nurture their Jewishness in secret. As Peter Berek puts it, since at this time no one could live openly as a Jew in England, Jewishness was by definition 'a covert state, a state that entailed multiple creeds, nationalities, even names'.[31] Jews became synonymous with dissimulation, in fact, they were seen to be most themselves when pretending to be someone else. Such a view was not generated by fears about conversion in the early modern period, but had older roots: according to a medieval Latin translation of an Arab Christian document, 'a Jew is not a Jew until he converts to Islam'. This rather confusing statement does not merely associate Jews and Muslims but also suggests that Jews most carefully preserve their identity when they have converted to another religion.[32] These are the multiple contexts which shape the image of Shylock as a devil that can put on a 'goodly show'.

Matters were further complicated by the fact that Jews, as one contemporary writer put it, 'have not for their mansion, any peculiar country, but are dispersed abroad among foreign nations'.[33] Jews could be Spanish, or Portuguese, or Russian, Turkish, and also, English, and early modern writings abound with categories such as 'an English Jew', or 'a Turkish Jew', which heightened confusion about whether Jewishness was a nationality, a religion, or a race. Jewishness was widely associated with the ability to assume a disguise. Shapiro recounts the story of a Jew converted to Christianity by Sir James Lancaster and taken to India. A Frenchman, Pyrard de Laval, who met Lancaster and this servant later noted that the latter 'was a Jew in faith and race, and knew a large number of languages'; with 'the English he was of their religion; with the Mahometans, of theirs, whereas all the while a Jew'.[34] The attempts to attribute hooked noses or a particular smell or a darker skin to Jews tell us that, as with the Irish, the lack of clear-cut distinctions between Jews and Christians were worrying to many English people. Portia's question, 'Which is the Merchant here and which the Jew' thus touches an exposed cultural nerve. It also touches a raw economic nerve, as we shall now examine.

Old Gods and New

Karl Marx dated the birth of capitalism in Europe to the sixteenth century; he explained that in pre-capitalist Europe, two groups of people could generate money that could function 'as capital' (or money that could be used to generate more money). These were usurers and merchants; their money was

prevented from turning into industrial capital by the feudal organization of the countryside and the guild organization of the towns. These fetters vanished with the dissolution of the feudal bands of retainers, and the expropriation and partial eviction of the rural population. The new manufactures were established at sea-ports, or at points in the countryside which were beyond the old municipalities and their guilds. Hence in England, the bitter struggle of the corporate towns against these new seed beds of industry.[35]

Historically, merchants were the most prominent moneylenders, and could be Christians as well as Jews. England had modified its usury statutes in 1571 and 1624, so moneylending per se was no longer proscribed, although the charging of excessively high interest rates was. Shakespeare's own father was among those prosecuted for charging unfair interest.[36] Thomas Wilson's *A Discourse Upon Usury* suggested that there were 'fewer usurers elsewhere than are here in England', and that usury was more 'outrageous . . . here in England than in any place else that I know in Christendom'.[37] Jews and Christians were competitors with overlapping activities and aspirations, both in England and elsewhere. In Italy, Jewish moneylenders offered stiff competition to Christian banks, which were set up in order to undercut the former. And in the Mediterranean, as we have already noted, much of the trade English merchants aspired to was in Jewish hands.

Shakespeare's play rewrites these rivalries by crafting a tension between usury and mercantile activity, and by racializing this tension. Shylock and the other Jews do not trade in anything but money, and no Christian in the play lends money for interest; Shylock says he hates Antonio both for being a Christian, and because he 'lends out money gratis', thus bringing down the rate of interest (1.3.40–2). The difference between usury and trade hinges upon how each generates its profits; whereas trade claims to be an exchange of goods between two parties for mutual benefit, usury uses money to generate more money and is premised upon the asymmetrical needs of the parties involved. In the play, moreover, Antonio's ships range the world and generate profit from worlds that lie far away from Venice. In contrast, Shylock is seen as a 'carrion crow' preying upon the very city that feeds him. Trade is thus portrayed as outward-looking, glamorous, and adventurous, and usury as inward-looking and cannibalistic. Not just that, but Shylock's moneylending paradoxically involves a movement away from the exchange of money; Walter Cohen reminds us that Shylock is demonized not because he indulges in usury but because he refuses to be paid in cash, and insists on Antonio's flesh. Therefore he becomes someone who is not just inward-looking, but backward, primitive, and irrational in his desires.[38]

Karl Marx famously read Jews as the very embodiment of capitalism; often, critics have interpreted Shylock along similar lines. But whereas Marx did not go on to suggest that Christians were anti-capitalist because they were anti-Semitic, some critics have been tempted to interpret the Christians of Shakespeare's play as representatives of a feudal order hostile to a newer order.[39] At one level, Antonio's ability to spend money he does not even possess, his distaste for taking interest, and his association with the gentlemanly Bassanio and the wealthy Portia (both of whom are lavish in their spending), smack of a feudal, princely ethos. But Walter Cohen rightly points out that it is Shylock who represents an older Jewish financial network, and Antonio who is the Christian merchant on the rise who needs to break into it: 'Both the characterization and the outcome of *The Merchant Of Venice* mark Antonio as the harbinger of modern capitalism' (771). And yet, as Theodore B. Leinwand cautions, Antonio is extremely uneasy about this role. He has borrowed money from others besides Shylock, and lent money to many people, including Bassanio; therefore he is 'thoroughly locked into early modern credit relations'. Leinwand suggests that Antonio's mysterious sadness, with which the play opens, is a symptom of his alienation from his role in Venetian finance and foreign trade; repeatedly, though vainly, Antonio tries to 'distance himself from financial operations' in the play.[40]

Antonio's is a genteel mercantilism, which combines the values of a bygone world with the daring and risk-taking required in the new. His ships are spoken of as 'argosies' which tower over 'the petty traffickers' who acknowledge their superiority and 'do them reverence' (1.1.9–13). His 'venturing', like the exploits of Drake and Ralegh, can be presented as an individual, honourable enterprise, far removed from the collective profit-seeking of the joint-stock companies, in whose hands foreign trade was beginning to concentrate. Thus, in many ways, Antonio is also 'faced backward in history'.[41] Shylock, we have already noted, is in some aspects a figure from the past, a resurrection of the medieval stereotype of the Jew, who is unable to divorce his economic transactions from his racial antipathy. In this way the antipathy between Christian and Jew is infused with an older, folkloric aspect, epitomized by the bond of a pound of flesh. Shakespeare is reminding us that contemporary economic rivalries were built upon a long and complicated history of antagonisms fought on a shared terrain.

In reality, private venturing such as Antonio's was not counterposed to, but contributed to the formation of large overseas trading companies, such as the English East India Company, which was established in 1600.[42] Antonio's ships are bound to Tripoli, to 'the Indies', Mexico, Lisbon, Barbary, and England. At this time Venetian ships did not trade across the Atlantic or the Indian Ocean, but all over Europe, including in England, there was an excitement about the endless possibilities of such far-flung markets. With the so-called discovery of the New World and rediscovery of the Old, Europe imagined itself uniquely positioned at the heart of the known world; as one resident of Seville remarked, 'previously our regions... used to be at the very end of the world, but now, with the discovery of the Indies, they have become its centre'.[43] In England, which, compared to many other European powers, was a latecomer to both trade and colonization, the benefits of foreign trade were ardently advocated by men such as Richard Eden and Richard Hakluyt. Samuel Purchas's massive travel collection *Hakluytus Posthumus* opens with a statement of international variety:

It is true that as every member of the bodie hath somewhat eminent, whereby it is serviceable to the whole; so every Region excelleth all others in some Peculiar Raritie, which may be termed extraordinary respectively, though otherwise most common and ordinary in its owne place…and so each part is to the other part in some or other part, and particular respect admirable.[44]

On this variety and mutual need rests the justification for trade. However, even Purchas must acknowledge the hierarchies that actually structure intercontinental relations: 'Asia, Africa and America have been discovered to our Reader, not as enjoying the first and best place, but offering their ready service and best attendance unto Europe.'[45] In the long term, European trade could not have attained its powerful global position without the systematic colonial plunder that was absolutely crucial for the birth of capitalism; as Marx noted:

The colonial system ripened trade and navigation as in a hothouse…The discovery of gold and silver in America, the extirpation, enslavement and entombment in mines of the indigenous population of that continent, the beginnings of the conquest and plunder of India, and the conversion of Africa into a preserve for the commercial hunting of blackskins, are all things which characterize the dawn of the era of capitalist production…[46]

Written at a time when these processes had only just been set in motion, Shakespeare's play captures both the excitement and the unease they generated.

Although Marx points to the 'Christian character' of the European 'primitive accumulation' (or the way in which Europe accumulated the wealth that made capitalism possible), for him, the colonial system was a ' "strange God" who perched himself side by side with the old divinities of Europe on the altar, and one fine day threw them all overboard with a shove and a kick. It proclaimed the making of profit as the ultimate and sole purpose of mankind.' Thus, in Marx's view, while colonial exploitation was essential for Europe's transition to capitalism, both colonialism and capitalism could only proceed by getting rid of older prejudices. Elsewhere, Marx appropriated Shakespeare to make his point that money was the new god who would eliminate the older deities of Europe. He cited the following passage from Shakespeare's *Timon of Athens* in which Timon, abandoned by his friends after he has lost his wealth, bitterly concludes that money can transform everything into its opposite:

> make
> Black white, foul fair, wrong right,
> Base noble, old young, coward valiant
>
> .   .   .   .   .
>
> This yellow slave
> Will knit and break religions, bless th'accurs'd,
> Make the hoar leprosy adored, place thieves,
> And give them title, knee, and approbation
> With senators on the bench.

(4.3.28–38)

For Timon, 'yellow glittering gold' is simultaneously a 'visible god' and a 'slave', powerful precisely because it is so obedient. He suggests that money has the power to displace religion; Marx quotes the passage while observing that because every commodity can be exchanged for money, money is a 'radical leveller, it extinguishes all distinctions'.[47]

However, *The Merchant of Venice* makes clear that the making of money *exacerbates* religious differences, rather than undermining them. In this play, we can trace a different dynamic from the one outlined by Marx, one of the appropriation and transformation, rather than the elimination, of the 'old divinities' by the new. The play presents Jewish-Christian strife by evoking older tropes and motifs, yet in doing so, it conveys not the past but the evolving present of economic and race relations. And indeed, as analysts of race now emphasize, it was in the better interests of capitalism and colonialism *not* to discard older social structures entirely. Slavery, for example, with which Shylock charges Venetian Christians, was a pre-capitalist practice, but one which was not merely retained, but systematized and expanded by colonialism. In the play, it is precisely Venice's economic dependence upon those who are considered outsiders that generates unease and a hardening of attitudes, an antipathy that is articulated as racial. In economic terms as well as somatic, it is hard to tell the Merchant from the Jew—because their terrain is shared, the combat is racially charged.

The Merchant of Venice 'resolves' the problem of Venetian dependence upon Shylock's wealth by ensuring that the latter is transferred
into Christian hands. This resolution hinges upon Jessica's conversion to Christianity, for she takes some of his money with her, while
the rest comes to her and Lorenzo as a result of Portia's courtroom
victory over Shylock. But the transfer of wealth is not enough, for
Antonio also demands that Shylock convert to Christianity. This
demand seems to be simultaneously excessive and regressive, a throw-
back to an antipathy that should have no place in a 'modern' mercantile system. Along with the fact that Venice brands Shylock an 'alien',
the demand for his conversion most powerfully conveys the fact that
new gods do not displace the old. We have already discussed how in
various dramatic texts of the period, conversion is presented as a fair
exchange of Christian faith for non-Christian wealth. The converts
themselves say so, and imagine that conversion erases their difference.
In *The Merchant of Venice*, Shylock's unwillingness to become a
Christian offers us a very different perspective. It reminds us that
even though conversion appears to be an invitation to assimilate, it is
actually a way of asserting social power. Thus, if the new gods of
capitalism and colonialism seek to erode the old differences, they do
so coercively, and in ways that intensify existing hierarchies. In this
play we see that a language of sharing and community can actually be
used to articulate hostility, as when Shylock makes a passionate claim
to a shared humanity, which is actually part of his argument for
retribution:

Hath not a Jew eyes? Hath not a Jew hands, organs, dimensions, senses,
affections, passions...if you prick us do we not bleed? If you tickle us do we
not laugh? If you poison us do we not die? And if you wrong us shall we not
revenge? (3.1.54–62)

Similarly, Shylock's conversion indicates not universal brotherhood
but his marginalization from Christian society.

Jessica's Difference

We began this chapter by discussing the spectre of Christian miscegenation with both Jews and blacks that haunts *The Merchant of
Venice*. As we have seen, the play does not treat them as equivalent.

Jessica's conversion highlights the fact that the pregnant Moor is not converted, but it also needs to be contrasted with the forced conversion of Shylock in order to understand how gender complicates issues of race and religion.[48]

The very first time we see Jessica, she expresses her alienation from her father and his house which she describes as 'hell'; she follows this with an assertion that although she is daughter to Shylock's 'blood', she is not to his 'manners' (2.3.19). Here she suggests that in her own case, 'blood' can be divorced from 'manners', whereas in Shylock's case, they cannot. As Mary Janell Metzger shows, 'Jessica's incorporation into Christian society is essential to defining her father's alien status'; this incorporation depends not only on Jessica's fairness but also her eagerness to cross the very boundaries which her father has reinforced with his hatred of Christians.[49] Throughout the play, Jessica's Christian admirers emphasize both her fairness and her tractability: she is 'sweet Jew' (2.3.11), 'gentle Jessica' (2.4.19), 'fair Jessica' (2.4.28); she is 'wise, fair, and true' (2.6.56). Finally, when Shylock claims her as his 'flesh and blood', Salerio retorts: 'There is more difference between thy flesh and hers than between jet and ivory; more between your bloods than there is between red wine and Rhenish' (3.1.35–7). The difference between Jessica and Shylock is thus translated into one of colour—they are cast as literally black and white in relation to one another.

A similar difference between men and women was suggested in relation to other parts of the world. Peter Heylyn's *Microcosmus* observed that in Macedonia, 'the men are of the African complexion and language...the women fair but hating company and going covered'.[50] Bartolemé Argensola's history of the Moluccan islands, on which Fletcher's play *The Island Princess* was based, claimed that the 'Natives Differ from one another, as it were through a Miraculous Bounty of Nature, for it has made the Women Fair and Beautiful, and the Men, of a darker Colour than Quince'.[51] Fletcher's play attributes fairness exclusively to the Moluccan Princess Quisara who is to be converted to Christianity and married to the play's Portuguese hero. In fact all of the converted women on the Renaissance stage are remarkably fair, and their skin colour is essential to their convertibility. As mentioned earlier, these conversions hark back to a long literary tradition featuring a converted Saracen princess. The figure of the converted Jewess reinforces the striking parallels between Muslims and Jews. While in *The Merchant of Venice*, as in these other plays, the converted lady's whiteness is crucial, the most obvious difference between Shylock's flesh and Jessica's is that he is circumcized. Thus we can say that circumcision morphs into skin colour, and the uncircumcized female body is imagined as literally fairer than the circumcized male one.

It is also striking that, unlike the Muslim women who convert in other Renaissance plays, and unlike the figures in the civic pageants, Jessica does not express any religious zeal towards her new faith, although like them, she does ensure a transfer of money to Christian hands. *The Merchant* is also different from these other plays in one other respect—it does not end with conversion and marriage but allows us to see their after-effects. As the play proceeds, Jessica's conversion does not appear to have resulted in a fairy-tale ending; Launcelot's teasing suggests that marriage and conversion have been unable to save Jessica from the damnation her lineage confers upon her. Jessica's banter with Lorenzo invokes images of the tragic loves of Troilus and Cressida, Pyramus and Thisbe, Aeneas and Dido, Jason and Medea, at least three of which involved crossing the boundaries of community; she also suggests, even if jokingly, that Lorenzo's vows of faith included 'ne'er a true one' (5.1.20). Conversely Lorenzo calls Jessica's love 'unthrift', reminding the audience that she has squandered away much of Shylock's wealth, including exchanging her mother's ring for a monkey. Metzger concludes that while Jessica's desire to convert is essential to establishing Shylock's stubborn resistance to Christianity, its own uncertain outcome reinforces the idea of a Jewish difference which cannot be easily erased. There is thus both a crucial difference between father and daughter, and a shared inheritance that is immutable. We can extend this reading by suggesting that the unsuccessful attempts of other outsiders in the play to cross racial, national, and religious boundaries throw into relief Jessica's exceptional status, but simultaneously they also reinforce the uneasy note on which her story ends.

Finally, the difficulty of Jessica's conversion is also underlined by Portia's use of this term; she tells Bassanio, 'Myself and what is mine to you and yours | Is now converted' (3.2.166–7). By drawing attention to the fact that all marriages call upon women to be converted into new households and communities, Shakespeare highlights the range of differences within women. Morocco compares Portia to a contemporary coin, an 'angel'; and critics have pointed out that she is crucial to developing the economic as well as emotional relationships between men in this play. If Shylock's money, borrowed by Antonio, makes it possible for Bassanio to woo her, she first offers to repay Shylock many times over, and then saves Antonio's life by outwitting him. The friendship and love between Antonio and Bassanio is thus protected by Portia, even though she ensures that her own position as Bassanio's wife is not threatened by this love—by the end of the play Antonio, 'stand(s) indebted over and above | In love and service' to her 'evermore' (4.1.410–11).[52] Portia establishes this emotional and financial community by refusing to circulate beyond a closed cultural conduit. That is why her repudiation of Morocco and Aragon are not just aberrations on the part of an otherwise genteel maiden, but an essential part of her gentility and value within the economy of the play.

Historically, marriages between Christians, Jews, and Muslims had been taboo for centuries. Between the eleventh and fourteenth centuries, any sexual contact between Christian and non-Christians was deemed impermissible by canon law.[53] In each community the punishment for sexual transgression was always worse for women. The requirement that Jews and Muslims should dress differently from Christians partly arose from the fear that the physical similarities between these groups would lead to sexual intercourse between them. Here, Muslim women risked enslavement by consorting with Christian men, but a Jewish woman in the same position would be fined, even mutilated rather than enslaved. In England where the population had not been so heterogeneous, fears of miscegenation heightened as overseas contact spread, and thirteenth-century laws forbidding intermarriage between Jews and Christians were reiterated in the seventeenth century.[54] The supposition that non-Christian women desire white and Christian men also increased: Jewish women, writes Thomas Browne, 'desire copulation' with Christians 'rather than [with] their own nation and affect Christian carnality above circumcised venery', an idea which is repeated by Bulwer's *Anthropometamorphoses* a few years later.[55] As in Shakespeare's play, in these writings, the active desire of non-Christian women for Christian men is evoked in order to define the boundaries of culture.

Samuel Purchas had compared Jewish usury to female prostitution, complaining that in Italy 'the beastly trade of courtesans and cruel trade of Jews is suffered for gain'; the Pope grants them a 'subsidy for ten thousand crowns... So well is the rule of Paul observed by this Bishop not to be a lover of filthy lucre, from filthy stews, from filthy Jews'.[56] Here Purchas implies that borrowing money is a form of having sex. In *The Merchant of Venice* Christians not only have metaphoric sex by borrowing money from Jews, but also have actual sex with Jews, which also results in the flow of money from Jewish to Christian hands. Jewish conversions to Christianity, the careful sifting between permissible and impermissible sexualities, voluntary and enforced conversions, all address the anxieties provoked by monetary and sexual traffic. However, as we have seen, the play has no safe or neat answers to these large cultural worries. But by dramatically yoking together questions of religious and sexual conversion with those of trade, it allows us to see how economic rivalries and interactions helped harden religious differences into racial ones, and, conversely, how race is crucial to the economic transformation of Europe. Finally, *The Merchant of Venice* demonstrates that race was never solely attached to skin colour, but also that skin colour was never too far from any articulation of race.

Playing with Shakespeare

Shakespeare's last play, *The Tempest* (1611), is the one most widely and most controversially linked to issues of colonialism and race. Until the 1980s, critics routinely classified the play as a romance, as Shakespeare's valedictory tribute to the power of art and theatre. But outside the Western (and colonial) academy, the events on the remote island where the exiled Duke of Milan, Prospero, brings up his daughter Miranda, and re-establishes sovereignty by mastering the airy spirit Ariel, the savage native Caliban, and eventually his ship-wrecked brother and his companions, had been interpreted quite differently. Swept up by the urgencies of decolonization, a host of intellectuals, novelists, playwrights, performers, and activists contested, appropriated, celebrated, and fought over the play as a parable of colonial relations. For them Prospero and Caliban became emblematic of the colonial master and colonized subject; they could not, as most literary critics of their time tended to do, read Prospero as wisdom without cruelty, or Caliban as monstrosity without humanity.

Ironically, these anti-colonial appropriations did not ponder over the nature of sixteenth- and seventeenth-century contact between Europeans and non-Europeans, or the specific histories and geographies with which the play conversed. On the other hand, even those critics who were reluctant to read the play in purely colonial terms admitted that it drew upon materials pertaining to European contact with the Americas, especially reports of an English shipwreck off the Bermuda islands and the French humanist Montaigne's essay 'Of Cannibals'. The 'Bermuda pamphlets' discussed how the hardships they endured, as well as natural abundance of the New World, had an impact upon the surviving crew, who became both lazy and rebellious. When these men finally made it to the recently established English plantation at Jamestown, they discovered chaos among the settlers, as well as a breakdown of their relations with the native Indians. *The Tempest*'s reflection upon the effect of island life upon different Europeans, and their relationship to previous inhabitants, seems at least tangentially inspired by these pamphlets, as well as by Montaigne's essay. This essay meditates upon difference between Europeans and the inhabitants of 'that other world which has been discovered in our century'.[1] It suggests that the inhabitants of the newly discovered 'boundless country' are like the fruits of Nature, among whom there is

no sort of traffic, no knowledge of letters, no science of numbers, no name of a magistrate or for political superiority, no custom of servitude, no riches or poverty, no contracts, no successions, no partitions, no occupations but leisure ones, no care for any but common kinship, no clothes, no agriculture, no metal, no use of wine or wheat... They are not fighting for the conquest of new lands, for they still enjoy that natural abundance that provides them without toil and trouble with all things necessary in such profusion that they have no wish to enlarge their boundaries... (153, 156)

It was Europeans, Montaigne suggested, who were both *unnatural* and unwilling to recognize that, being confident in their own superiority. In Shakespeare's play, the island inspires old Gonzalo to the vision of a similar 'commonwealth' where there will be 'no kind of traffic', 'no name of magistrate', where

> Letters should not be known; riches, poverty,
> And use of service, none; contract, succession,
> Bourn, bound of land, tilth, vineyard, none;
> No use of metal, corn, or wine, or oil;
> No occupation, all men idle, all.
>
> (2.1.156–60)

This association of savages with primordial nature was not always read as an index of their innocence and goodness; rather, as Montaigne suggests, it usually signified the inferiority of the inhabitants of the New World, and their being versions of the uncivilized and brutish wild men of medieval legends. If Gonzalo conjures up Montaigne's view, Caliban personifies the other, more common approach; he is, Prospero alleges, 'a born devil, on whose nature | Nurture can never stick' (4.1.188–9). He is a 'natural' man who simply cannot be civilized or assimilated into culture. Miranda suggests otherwise, pointing out that Caliban does learn his master's language. But, she says, there is a quality in him which makes him irreducibly different: 'thy vile race... had that in't which good natures | Could not abide to be with' (1.2.360–2). Thus she reverses Montaigne's terms by associating 'good natures' with Europeans, and Caliban with an uncivilized but far from innocent, monstrous 'race'.

It was not until the mid-1980s that a series of influential critical essays suggested the ways in which *The Tempest* offered a sustained reflection upon the violence, the asymmetry, as well as the intimacy of the colonial encounter.[2] To some extent, critics were simply catching up with and complicating the debate that had been inaugurated outside the academy. In the wake of anti-colonial uprisings in Madagascar, Octavio Mannoni had read the play to suggest that all colonized peoples suffer, like Caliban, from a 'dependency complex', which is to say that they need the firm hand of the ruler to keep them from insanity.[3] This view was contested by a host of Caribbean writers and intellectuals—Roberto Fernandez Retamar appropriated Caliban as a symbol of the oppression as well as rebellion of the Americas against colonialism.[4] Aimé Césaire drew upon Caribbean anti-colonial struggles as well as the Black Power movement in the USA in his play *Une Tempête* (*A Tempest*), to picture a resistant and highly articulate Caliban who, unlike his counterpart in Shakespeare's play, does not need Prospero's gift of language in order to curse.[5] Frantz Fanon's book *Black Skin, White Masks* had also countered Mannoni's dependency complex by suggesting that it is colonial rule that imposes a psychic conflict upon colonized peoples, who are constantly torn between colonial values and their native inheritance.[6] Earlier, the Barbadian novelist George Lamming had situated himself as a Caliban figure who uses his colonial English education to raise his voice against colonial oppression.[7]

These (and many more) Caribbean intellectuals interacted with each other, and with the imperatives of decolonization via *The Tempest*. They also grappled with the politics of race in the Americas, interpreting Caliban variously as a symbol of black power and as a hybrid typifying the 'mestizaje' or racial intermixture of the region. Ariel was once read as the appropriate symbol of the mixture and intermingling of races in America but was cast by Césaire as a mulatto who compromises with white colonial power. Only some of these writers, like Césaire and Lamming, really engaged at any length with Shakespeare's play; for many others, it was simply a powerful cultural symbol to be seized and used for their own ends. The play also inspired divergent opinions on the extent to which colonialism violated native languages and cultures, and on the possibility of colonized people recovering their earlier traditions in order to 'curse' colonial authorities and liberate themselves. Césaire suggests that colonized people can and must reach back to their indigenous roots whereas Lamming takes more precise note of the ways in which Western education shapes the colonized subject, and must be deliberately shaken off as well as utilized by him. Like the other writers mentioned here, he does not consider a female anti-colonial subject and her possible interactions with the play; indeed *The Tempest* is notoriously difficult to appropriate from a feminist perspective.[8]

Lamming and others were far ahead of the Shakespearian scholarship of their day.[9] The linguistic and cultural aspects of colonialism highlighted by them later became central to postcolonial debates about resistance, but also, more specifically, about early modern colonial encounters and *The Tempest*. Stephen Greenblatt's work has been the most significant here; Greenblatt points out that two apparently contradictory ideologies about language were used to secure European domination. On the one hand, European colonists strenuously refused to acknowledge the literacy and cultures of America, and spoke of natives as wild people outside the pale of civil society. On the other, documents like the Spanish *Requerimeinto*, which was drawn up in 1513 to announce to the natives that if they did not convert to Christianity and obey the Spanish monarchs they would be dispossessed and enslaved, assumed that the natives could understand the European announcements and had been fairly warned about the consequences of disobeying them:

Though they seem to be opposite extremes, both positions reflect a fundamental inability to sustain the simultaneous perception of likeness and difference...they either push the Indians towards utter difference—and thus silence—or towards utter likeness—and thus the collapse of their own unique identity.[10]

Thus ideas of both sameness and difference were pressed into colonial service, just as they were also useful strategies for anti-colonial articulation.

While literary critics have paid more attention to the early modern aspects of the colonial encounter, and the anti-colonial appropriations have picked up on the dynamics of nineteenth- and twentieth-century colonialism and imperialism, both have privileged America as the site of colonial conflict.[11] Both have also offered the encounter between a lettered Prospero and an unlettered Caliban as emblematic of not just an American reality but of colonial relations per se. This has been less problematic in the case of the appropriations because they address a later period in history when in large parts of the colonized world the European presence had decimated, or at least marginalized and eroded native cultures. Thus it was possible during the heyday of anti-imperialist movements for Caliban to be generalized into a potent symbol of the disenfranchised natives of not just America, but also Africa and Asia.

Of course this plasticity has its problems, and for many anti-colonial and postcolonial writers, Caliban is not an adequate symbol of their oppression or revolt. But to privilege America in understanding the play's moment of origin is perhaps even more limiting. Critical focus on New World encounters was rewarding and important in drawing attention to early modern colonial and racial discourses, but it tended to obscure other encounters such as those between European Christians and Turks, Africans, Jews, or Indians. These other encounters, as we have seen throughout this book, were part of a long and complicated history of interaction. Europeans could not interpret them simply as the clash between lettered and unlettered societies, or a meeting of the civilized and savage, culture and nature. Therefore the Caliban–Prospero relationship needs always to be set against other representations, rather than taken as symbolizing the entire encounter between Europe and its 'others'.[12]

Recent critics have also suggested that an exclusively American focus narrows, not just our view of early modern race and colonialism as a whole, but also the geographies and histories that resonate with *The Tempest*. The play speaks to Mediterranean, North African, and Irish, as well as Atlantic contexts, often moving between these different regions. A New World focus cannot, for example, make sense of the curious exchange (in Act 2, scene 1) among Alonzo's retinue concerning his daughter Claribel. The courtiers discuss how they were shipwrecked while returning from 'Afric', where Claribel was married to the king of Tunis. Sebastian compares Claribel to 'widow Dido' evoking not Virgil's version of the story of Dido, queen of Carthage, where she is an African queen abandoned by Aeneas, but an older one where she was a virtuous widow who resisted the advances of an African.[13] But the comparison turns on a contrast—whereas Dido resisted the African, Claribel's father 'would not bless our Europe with your daughter, | But rather loose her to an African' (2.1.130–1). For this, Sebastian suggests, Alonzo is now being punished by the shipwreck and additional loss of his son. As Jerry Brotton reminds us, 'the voyage undertaken by Alonzo and his retinue from Naples to Tunis was a voyage that traversed one of the most contested stretches of water within the Mediterranean world'.[14]

Leo Africanus describes how the 'mighty city of Tunis' was built upon the ruins of ancient Carthage, and how its monarch was 'saluted king of all Africa, because indeed there was no prince of Africa at the same time comparable unto him'.[15] Africanus also points to the centrality of Tunis, where 'Genoueses, Venetians and other Christian merchants resort and...repose themselves out of the tumult and concourse of the Moors', to the early modern Europe. The English were both passionately interested and frustratingly marginalized in this region. This is why, Brotton suggests, the play erases the Ottoman presence in the region in order to offer 'a conveniently imprecise but sanitized version of the Mediterranean World' which could allow Englishmen to gloss over their marginalization and look forward to a different enterprise in the Americas (37). But does the play in fact hark back to an older geography of the region in order to eliminate its contemporary tensions? After all, Claribel's story plays upon the imagined as well as real encounters between white European women and Moors which, as we have seen, reverberated through early modern culture.[16] The figure of Caliban's mother Sycorax, 'the damned witch', who Prospero says was banished 'for mischiefs manifold and sorceries terrible' to the island from Algiers, returns us again to contemporary North African geography, and to the fears evoked by African and Moorish femininity. Unlike the fair Moorish women who can be converted and assimilated into European families, this 'hag' from

Algiers must be eliminated and detached from her child, who can then be adopted as the white man's burden, acknowledged by Prospero as a 'thing of darkness' who is both alien and 'mine'. Thus, if the play envisions a colonial dynamic in the New World, it does so by simultaneously registering the power and threat of the Old.

And even this complicated interaction between the Atlantic and Mediterranean geographies and histories does not exhaust the play's range of references. After all, its island could simply refer to England itself, where hierarchical relations between masters and serfs had been enforced by physical as well as ideological violence. Or it could be Ireland, another island where the English had rehearsed the strategies of colonial domination which they later employed in America.[17] The Irish case brings together aspects of both New World and Old World encounters, for in medieval as well as early modern writings, the Irish were both disparaged as brutish and unlettered and acknowledged to have a rich cultural heritage of their own. They needed mastery, and yet were a culture powerful enough to contaminate all potential colonists. The multiplicity of locations that can be read into the play also indicates the historical interconnections *between* different encounters—the Irish experience, according to some historians, prepared the English for their American forays, while according to others, attitudes to native Americans coloured English opinions about Moors. Thus, the multiple valences of *The Tempest* remind us of the global connections inaugurated by colonialism.

They also remind us that literary texts play with the vocabularies they inherit, transforming them as they do so. For example, Shakespeare uses the word 'gaberdine' in relation to both Shylock (1.3.111) and Caliban (2.2.37). Each usage indicates the specific histories of clothing as a marker of Jewish or Irish difference, but their overlap also indicates that the theatre often takes liberties with these specific histories. Recently it has been suggested that negative stereotypes about racial 'others' were created and disseminated by literature, and especially by the theatre.[18] While I cannot agree, it is true that the theatre did not simply repeat but also created images of race and difference, images that were then powerful enough to percolate down to and shape later histories of difference. Many of these images were not just stereotypes, though some certainly were. Some were reduced into types by later histories of interpretation and staging. For example, Shakespeare does not tell us anything about Caliban's skin colour, but in the nineteenth and twentieth centuries, Caliban's blackness was taken for granted, both by his champions and by those who read him as a monster, because colonial history had made blackness synonymous with bondage and inferiority. For the same reason, Othello's blackness was constantly contested and qualified. Both Caliban and Othello were originally shaped by multiple histories of contact, several overlapping and competing notions of difference. Perhaps that is why these figures remained culturally available for centuries as images that could be interpreted in a variety of ways, though often these interpretations narrowed and restricted their original resonance.

At the beginning of this book I suggested that representations of difference are crucial for any culture's self-definition, and that early modern descriptions and dramatizations of various Indians and Moors provided a language in which a fast-expanding Europe redefined itself. It is, then, ironic that the colonized peoples have not always challenged Shakespeare's representations of racial difference; occasionally they have also appropriated such representations as a vocabulary they can use to contest colonial dynamics. But the history of Caribbean interactions with *The Tempest* reminds us that such appropriations also go beyond Shakespeare, and reach out to aspects of non-European cultures and histories that are not registered by European texts. They remind us that we too need to look beyond Shakespeare's images of race and colonialism, to discover what these cultures were doing and saying about Europe and about themselves. This, I believe, is the next important task for Shakespearians and other scholars of early modern Europe. The effort will require multiple linguistic and other archival skills, but more importantly, it will require adjusting our conceptual framework to acknowledge the existence and the depth of these other societies and to remember that they shaped the world in which Shakespeare created his pictures of race and colonialism.

Notes

INTRODUCTION. RACE AND COLONIALISM IN THE STUDY OF SHAKESPEARE

1. Bloke Modisane, *Blame Me on History* (New York, 1963), 167–8, 70.
2. Quoted by Peter Erickson, 'Representations of Blacks in the Renaissance', *Criticism* 35: 4 (Fall 1993), 522.
3. Michael Bamshad *et al.*, 'Genetic Evidence on the Origins of Indian Caste Populations', *Genome Research* 11: 6 (June 2001), 994–1004, 991.
4. Thomas Hahn, 'The Difference the Middle Ages Makes: Color and Race before the Modern World', *Journal of Medieval and Early Modern Studies* 31: 1 (2001), 1–37, 9.
5. Jared Diamond, 'Race without Color', *Discover* 15: 11 (1994), 83–9, 84.
6. Quoted by Rob Nixon, 'Caribbean and African Appropriations of *The Tempest*', *Critical Inquiry* 13 (1987), 558.
7. *Thomas Platter's Travels in England*, trans. Clare Williams (London, 1937), 170.
8. Thomas Newton, 'Epistle Dedicatory', in *The Notable History of Saracens* (London, 1575).
9. Edward W. Said, *Orientalism* (London, 1978).
10. Liah Greenfeld, *Nationalism: Five Roads to Modernity* (Cambridge, Mass., 1992), 67.
11. Stephen Greenblatt, *Renaissance Self-Fashioning: From More to Shakespeare* (Chicago, 1980), 9; *Marvellous Possessions: The Wonder of the New World* (Chicago, 1991).
12. Kim F. Hall, *Things of Darkness: Economies of Race and Gender in Early Modern England* (Ithaca, NY, 1995).
13. Valerie Traub, 'The Psychomorphology of the Clitoris', *GLQ* 2 (1995), 81–113.
14. Andrew Hadfield and Willy Maley, 'Introduction', in Brenden Bradshaw, Andrew Hadfield, and Willy Maley (eds.), *Representing Ireland: Literature and the Origins of Conflict* (Cambridge, 1993), 7.

15. James Shapiro, *Shakespeare and the Jews* (New York, 1996).

16. Benedict Anderson, *Imagined Communities, Reflections on the Origin and Spread of Nationalism* (London, 1991).

17. Quoted by Sharon Kinoshita '"Pagans are wrong and Christians are right": Alterity, Gender, and Nation in the *Chanson de Roland*', *Journal of Medieval and Early Modern Studies*, 31: 1 (2001), 79–111, 86–7.

18. See Greenfeld, *Nationalism*, 29–30, to which I am indebted here.

19. See Thomas J. Scanlon, *Colonial Writing and the New World 1583–1671: Allegories of Desire* (Cambridge, 1999).

20. Quoted by Andrew Hadfield, *Literature, Travel and Colonial Writing in the English Renaissance, 1545–1625* (Oxford, 1998), 104.

21. Sir John Burrough, quoted Robert Sencourt, *India in English Literature* (Port Washington, Wis., 1923), 50.

22. Sir Walter Ralegh, *The Discoverie of Guiana* ed. Neil L. Whitehead (Manchester, 1997), 136.

23. Edmund Spenser, *A View of the Present State of Ireland*, in Henry Morley (ed.), *Ireland under Elizabeth and James the First* (London, 1890), 54.

24. *Thomas Platter's Travels in England*, 171–2.

25. See Shapiro, *Shakespeare and the Jews*, 180–93.

26. Hans Kohn, 'The Genesis and Character of English Nationalism', *Journal of the History of Ideas*, 1 (Jan. 1940), 69–94, 73.

27. Eldred Jones, *Othello's Countrymen: The African in English Renaissance Drama* (London, 1965), 28.

28. Peter Berek, 'The Jew as Renaissance Man', *Renaissance Quarterly* 51: 1 (1998), 128–62, 130, 158.

29. Edmund Spenser, *Present State of Ireland*, 82.

CHAPTER I. THE VOCABULARIES OF RACE

1. The *OED* also lists some of the other meanings and usage discussed below; see also Michael Banton, *Racial Theories* (Cambridge, 1987), 1–27.

2. John Florio, *A Worlde of Wordes, or most copious, and exact Dictionarie in Italian and English* (London, 1598), 313.

3. Montaigne, 'Of glory', in *The Complete Essays of Montaigne*, trans. Donald M. Frame (Stanford, Calif., 1989), 475.

4. Edward Topsell, *The Historie of Four-Footed Beastes* (London, 1607), 298.

5. Sir Thomas Herbert, *A relation of some yeares travaile, begunne anno 1626* (London, 1634), 17.

6. Sir John Wynne, *The History of the Gwydir Family* (Oswestry, 1878), 20.

7. Peter Heylyn, *Microcosmus, or a little description of the great world* (Oxford, 1621), 194.

8. Ibid. 300; George Sandys, *A Relation of a Journey Begun, Anno Dom. 1610*, in Samuel Purchas, *Hakluytus Posthumus or Purchas His Pilgrimes* (Glasgow, 1905), viii. 171.

9. Henry Blount, *A Voyage into the Levant* (London, 1638), 2.

10. Fulcher of Chartres is quoted by Geraldine Heng, 'Cannibalism, the First Crusade, and the Genesis of Medieval Romance', *Differences* 10: 1 (1998), 98–174, 113.

11. See Sharon Kinoshita, 'The Politics of Courtly Love: *La Prise D'Orange* and the Conversion of the Saracen Queen', *Romanic Review* 86: 2 (1995), 265–87, 273.

12. St Augustine is quoted and discussed by Robert Bartlett, 'Medieval and Modern Concepts of Race and Ethnicity', *Journal of Medieval and Early Modern Studies* 31: 1 (2001), 39–56, 45.

13. Richard Hooker, *Of the Lawes of Ecclesiasticall Politie* (1554–97) (Menton, 1969), bk. 4, 154.

14. *The Poems of James VI of Scotland*, ed. James Craige, Scottish Text Society (Edinburgh, 1955), i. 202.

15. Reginald Scot, *Discovery of Witchcraft* (London, 1584), 535.

16. Quoted by Peter Fryer, *Staying Power: The History of Black People in Britain* (London, 1984), 136.

17. Edmund Spenser, *The Fairie Queene*, in *The Poeticall Works of Edmund Spenser*, ed. J. C. Smith and E. De Selincourt (London, 1912).

18. William Painter calls them a nation in *The Palace of Pleasure* (1567) ed. Joseph Jacob (London, 1890), 165; Fletcher speaks of 'a race of noble Amazons' in *The Woman's Prize* (2.2.925), *Comedies and Tragedies Written by Francis Beaumont and John Fletcher* (London, 1647).

19. Quoted by John Gillies, *Shakespeare and the Geography of Difference* (Cambridge, 1994), 74–5.

20. Sir Walter Ralegh, *The Discoverie of Guiana*, ed. Neil L. Whitehead (Manchester, 1997), 196.

21. Louis Adrian Montrose, 'The Work of Gender in the Discourse of Discovery', in Stephen Greenblatt (ed.), *New World Encounters* (Berkeley, 1993), 177–217.

22. See Nancy Leys Stepan, 'Race and Gender: The Role of Analogy in Science', in David Theo Goldberg (ed.), *The Anatomy of Racism* (Minneapolis, 1990), 38–57, 40.

23. Paul Freedman, *Images of the Medieval Peasant* (Stanford, Calif., 1994), 94.

24. 'The Travels and Most Miserable Captivity of William Davies' (1614), in Thomas Osborne, *A Collection of Voyages and Travels* (London, 1745), i. 484.

25. See Jennifer L. Morgan, '"Some Could Suckle over Their Shoulder": Male Travelers, Female Bodies, and the Gendering of Racial Ideology, 1500–1770', in *William and Mary Quarterly*, 3rd ser., 54: 1 (Jan. 1997), 167–91.

26. *The Masque of Blackness*, in *Ben Jonson: The Complete Masques*, ed. Stephen Orgel (New Haven, 1969), 50–1.

27. George Sandys, 'Relations of Africa', in Samuel Purchas, *Haklytus Posthumus*, vi. 213.

28. There is a vast scholarship on blackness in the theatre and the period in general. I have listed the most notable examples in the Further Reading.

29. Reginald Scot, *The Discovery of Witchcraft* (London, 1584), 152–3.

30. See Kim F. Hall, *Things of Darkness: Economies of Race and Gender in Early Modern England* (Ithaca, NY, 1995).

31. Robert Bartlett, *The Making of Europe: Conquest, Colonization and Cultural Change 950–1350* (Princeton, 1993), 197–9.

32. Étienne Balibar, 'Is There a Neo-racism?', in Étienne Balibar and Immanuel Wallerstein, *Race, Nation, Class: Ambiguous Identities* (London, 1991), 17–28, esp. 23.

33. James H. Sweet, 'The Iberian Roots of American Racist Thought', in *William and Mary Quarterly*, 3rd ser., 54: 1 (Jan. 1997), 143–66, 144.

34. Jerome Friedman, 'Jewish Conversion, the Spanish Pure Blood Laws and Reformation: A Revisionist View of Racial and Religious Anti-Semitism', *Sixteenth Century Journal* 18 (1987), 3–29.

35. Holinshed, *Chronicles* (London, 1587), v. 25. Samuel Purchas, *Hakluytus Posthumus*, i. 326–36.

36. Heylyn, *Microcosmus*, 400.

37. N. P. Canny, 'The Ideology of English Colonization: from Ireland to America', *William and Mary Quarterly*, 3rd ser., 30 (1973).

38. Andrew Hadfield, '"The naked and the dead": Elizabethan Perceptions of Ireland', in Jean-Pierre Maquerlot and Michèle Williams (eds.), *Travel and Drama in Shakespeare's Time* (Cambridge, 1996), 32–54, 41.

39. Ibid. 34–5.

40. John Bulwer, *Anthropometamorphoses, Man Transformed: or the Artificial Changeling* (London, 1653), 312.

41. Morgan, '"Some Could Suckle over Their Shoulder"', 167–92.

CHAPTER 2. RELIGION, COLOUR, AND RACIAL DIFFERENCE

1. 'The voyage and travell of M. Caesar Fredericke, Marchant of Venice into the East Indies', in Richard Hakluyt, *The Principal Navigations, Voyages, Traffiques and Discoveries of The English Nation* (Glasgow, 1903–5) v. 411.

2. Anthony Gerard Barthelemy, *Black Face, Maligned Race* (Baton Rouge, La., 1987), 6–17.

3. 'The second voyage to Guinea', in Hakluyt, *The Principal Navigations*, vi. 167, emphasis added.

4. 'Observations of Africa, taken out of John Leo', in Samuel Purchas, *Hakluytus Posthumus or Purchas His Pilgrimes* (Glasgow, 1905), v. 357.

5. Peter Fryer, *Staying Power: The History of Black People in Britain* (London, 1984), 8. See also Kim Hall, *Things of Darkness: Economies of Race and Gender in Early Modern England* (Ithaca, NY, 1995), 20.

6. Wolfram von Eschenbach, *Parzival*, trans. Helen M. Mustard and Charles E. Passage (New York, 1961), 26.

7. Francis Bacon, *New Atlantis*, in *Sylva Sylvarum or a Naturall History In Ten Centuries* (London, 1627), 26.

8. John Bulwer, *Anthropometamorphoses, Man Transformed: or the Artificial Changeling* (London, 1653), 401, 404.

9. Jean Bodin, *Method for the Easy Comprehension of History*, trans. Beatrice Reynolds (New York. 1945), 105.

10. 43 Elizabeth I (1601), in P. L. Hughes and J. F. Larkin, *Tudor Royal Proclamations*, iii (New Haven, 1969), 221.

11. Peter Heylyn, *Microcosmus or A little description of the whole world* (Oxford, 1621), 8.

12. Robert Burton, *The Anatomy of Melancholy* (first published 1621), ed. Floyd Dell and Paul Jordan-Smith (New York, 1927), 827.

13. Hakluyt, vii. 262.

14. Heylyn, *Microcosmus*, 403.

15. George Best, *A True Discourse of the Late Voyages of Discovery...* (London, 1578).

16. Paul Freedman, *Images of the Medieval Peasant* (Stanford, Calif., 1994), 94.

17. Discussed by Freedman, ibid. 87. See also Benjamin Braude, 'The Sons of Noah and the Construction of Ethnic and Geographical Identities in the Medieval and Early Modern periods', and James H. Sweet, 'The Iberian Roots of American Racist Thought', both in *William and Mary Quarterly*, 3rd ser., 54: 1 (1997), 103–42 and 143–66, esp. 149.

18. Thomas Calvert, *The Blessed Jew of Marocco or a Blackamoor Made White* (York, 1649).

19. See Lloyd E. Berry, 'Introduction', *The Geneva Bible*, a facsimile of the 1560 edn. (Madison, 1969), 20.

20. Thomas Palmer, *The Emblems of Thomas Palmer: Two Hundred Poosees*, ed. John Manning (New York, 1988).

21. Geffrey Whitney, *A Choice of Emblemes and Other Devices* (Aldershot, 1989).

22. See Hall, *Things of Darkness*, 85–107, to which I am indebted in this section.

23. Quoted and discussed by Kim Hall, ibid., 271.

24. Louise Olga Fradenburg, *City, Marriage, Tournament: Arts of Rule in Late Medieval Scotland* (Madison, 1991).

25. *The Song of Songs*, trans. Ariel Bloch and Chana Bloch (Berkeley, 1995), 47.

26. Thomas Hahn, 'The Difference the Middle Ages Makes: Color and Race before the Modern World', *Journal of Medieval and Early Modern Studies* 31: 1 (2001), 1–37, 23. See also Hall, *Things of Darkness*, 107–16.

27. Heylyn, *Microcosmus*, 371.

28. The story of the Queen of Sheba is narrated in 1 Kings 10. See James B. Pritchard (ed.), *Solomon and Sheba* (London, 1974).

29. Frances E. Dolan's essay, 'Taking the Pencil out of God's Hand: Art, Nature, and the Face-Painting Debate in Early Modern England', *PMLA* 108: 2 (1993), 224–39, offers a comprehensive analysis of the cosmetics controversy, but only briefly discusses its racial or colonial implications.

30. *The Complete Essays of Montaigne*, trans. Donald M. Frame (Stanford, Calif., 1989), 152.

31. James Shapiro, *Shakespeare and the Jews* (New York, 1996), 62.

32. Andrew Hess, *The Forgotten Frontier: A History of the Sixteenth Century Ibero-African Frontier* (Chicago, 1978), 151.

33. See especially Jerome Friedman, 'Jewish Conversion, the Spanish Pure Blood Laws and Reformation: A Revisionist View of Racial and Religious Anti-Semitism', *Sixteenth Century Journal* 18 (1987), 3–29.

34. Quoted Friedman, 'Jewish Conversion', 16–17.

35. Ibid. 17.

36. Edmund Spenser, *A View of the State of Ireland* in *Ireland Under Elizabeth and James the First*, ed. Henry Morley (London, 1890), 106.

37. Mary Stroll, *The Jewish Pope* (New York, 1987), 160, is quoted by Lisa Lampert, 'After Eden, Out of Zion: Defining the Christian in Early English Literature', Ph.D. thesis (University of California, Berkeley, 1996), p. ix.

38. Roger Williams, *Christenings Make not Christians* is quoted by Thomas Scanlan, *Colonial Writing and the New World 1583–1671* (Cambridge, 1999), 130.

39. Henry Byam, *A Returne from Argier* (London, 1628), 74.

40. Edward Kellet, *A Returne from Argier* (London, 1628), 3; emphasis added.

41. Ibid. 3; Thomas Dallam, *The Diary of Master Thomas Dallam* (1599–1600) repr. in *Early Voyages and Travels in the Levant*, ed. J. Theodore Bent (London, 1983), 79.

42. Hakluyt, *The Principal Navigations*, vi. 289.
43. Eldred D. Jones, *Elizabethan Image of Africa* (Washington, 1971), 35.
44. John Chamberlaine to Dudley Carleton, quoted Bernard Harris, 'A Portrait of a Moor', in (eds.), Catherine M. S. Alexander and Stanley Wells (eds.), *Shakespeare and Race* (Cambridge, 2000), 31.
45. John Phillips, *A Friendly Larum: Select Poetry Chiefly Devotional of the Reign of Queen Elizabeth*, ed. Edward Farr (Cambridge, 1845), pt. ii, 528.
46. Purchas, *Hakluytus Posthumus*, 314–19.
47. Nabil Matar, *Turks, Moors and Englishmen in the Age of Discovery* (New York 1999), 13.
48. George Peele, *The Battle of Alcazar* (London, 1594), Act 1, ll. 16–30. There are no scene divisions in this edition.

CHAPTER 3. WILDERNESS AND CIVILIZATION IN *TITUS ANDRONICUS*

1. Antony Sher and Gregory Doran, *Woza Shakespeare! Titus Andronicus in South Africa* (London, 1996), 213.
2. Review of the performance at the Britannia Theatre, Huxton, in Philip C. Kolin (ed.), *Titus Andronicus: Critical Essays* (New York, 1995), 377–9.
3. G. K. Hunter, 'Elizabethans and Foreigners', *Shakespeare Survey* 17 (1964), repr. in Catherine M. S. Alexander and Stanley Wells (eds.), *Shakespeare and Race* (Cambridge, 2000), 56.
4. John Gillies, *Shakespeare and the Geography of Difference* (Cambridge, 1994), 18.
5. See Jonathan Bate (ed.), *Titus Andronicus* (London, 1995); Anthony Brian Taylor, 'Lucius, the Severely Flawed Redeemer of *Titus Andronicus*', *Connotations* 6: 2 (1996/7), 138–53.
6. Jonathan Bate, '"Lucius, the Severely Flawed Redeemer of *Titus Andronicus*": A Reply', *Connotations* 6: 2 (1996/7), 332.
7. Philip C. Kolin, '"Lucius, the Severely Flawed Redeemer of *Titus Andronicus*": A Reply', *Connotations* 7: 1 (1997/8), 95–6.
8. Leslie A. Fiedler, 'Aaron', in Kolin (ed.), *Titus Andronicus: Critical Essays*, 160.
9. '"The Getting of a Lawful Race": Racial Discourse in Early Modern England and the Unrepresentable Black Woman', in Patricia Parker and Margo Hendricks (eds.), *Women, 'Race' and Writing in the Early Modern Period* (London, 1994), 41.
10. Dorothea Kehler, '"That Ravenous Tiger Tamora", *Titus Andronicus*'s Lusty Widow, Wife and M/Other', in Kolin (ed.), *Titus Andronicus: Critical Essays*, 317–32.

11. David E. Underdown, 'The Taming of the Scold: The Enforcement of Patriarchal Authority in Early Modern England', in Anthony Fletcher and John Stevensen (eds.), *Order and Disorder in Early Modern England* (Cambridge, 1985), 116–36.

12. Joan Kelly, 'Did Women Have a Renaissance?', in *Women, History, Theory* (Chicago, 1980), 19–50. See also Katherine Usher Henderson and Barbara F. Mcmanus (eds.), *Half Humankind* (Urbana, Ill., 1985); Natalie Zemon Davis and Arlette Farge (eds.), *A History Of Women: Renaissance and Enlightenment Paradoxes* (Cambridge, Mass., 1993).

13. *The Complete Essays of Montaigne*, trans. Donald M. Frame (Stanford, Calif., 1965), 675.

14. Daniel J. Vitkus, 'Turning Turk in *Othello*: The Conversion and Damnation of the Moor', *Shakespeare Quarterly* 48: 2 (Summer 1997), 145–76.

15. Reginald Scot, *The Discovery of Witchcraft* (1584), quoted by Eldred Jones, *Othello's Countrymen: The African in English Renaissance Drama* (London, 1965), 153.

16. Ibid. 153.

CHAPTER 4. *OTHELLO* AND THE RACIAL QUESTION

1. Henry Blount, *A Voyage into the Levant*, 3rd edn. (London, 1638), 2.

2. Dympna Callaghan, *Shakespeare Without Women, Representing Gender and Race on the Renaissance Stage* (London, 2000).

3. Robert Burton, *The Anatomy of Melancholy* (1621), ed. Floyd Dell and Paul Jordan-Smith (New York, 1927).

4. William Painter, *The Palace of Pleasure* (1567) (London, 1890), 197.

5. Richard Knolles, *General History of the Turks* (London, 1603), 350.

6. John Foxe, *Second Volume of the Ecclesiasticall History Containing the Acts and Monuments of Martyrs* (1563) (London, 1641), 992.

7. William Biddulph, *The Travels of Four Englishmen and a Preacher* (1612), in Thomas Osborne, *A Collection of Voyages and Travels*, i (London, 1745), 784–92.

8. *A True Relation of the Travels and Most Miserable Captivity of William Davies, Barber-Surgeon of London* (1614) in Osborne, *A Collection of Voyages and Travels*, 476.

9. Patricia Parker, 'Fantasies of "Race" and Gender, Africa, *Othello* and Bringing to Light', in Patricia Parker and Margo Hendricks (eds.), *Women, 'Race' and Writing* (London, 1994), 84–100, 95.

10. Leo Africanus, *The History and Description of Africa*, ed. Robert Brown (New York, 1906), 183.

11. Ania Loomba, *Gender, Race, Renaissance Drama* (Manchester, 1989), ch. 2.

12. See David C. McPherson, *Shakespeare, Jonson, and the Myth of Venice* (Newark, Del., 1990).

13. Roger Ascham, *The Schoolmaster* (London, 1579), 26.

14. Eric Griffin, 'Un-sainting James: Or, *Othello* and the "Spanish Spirits" of Shakespeare's Globe', *Representations* 62 (Spring 1998), 52–99.

15. Barbara Everett, 'Spanish *Othello*: The Making of Shakespeare's Moor', in Catherine M. S. Alexander and Stanley Wells (eds.), *Shakespeare and Race* (Cambridge, 2000), 64–81.

16. *A godly consultation unto the brethren and companyons of the Christian religyon* (Antwerp, 1542), fo. 6ᵛ.

17. Julia Reinhard Lupton, '*Othello* Circumcised: Shakespeare and the Pauline Discourse of Nations', *Representations* 57 (Winter 1997), 73–89.

18. Africanus, *The History and Description of Africa*, 105.

19. Jonathan Burton, '"A Most Wily Bird": Leo Africanus, *Othello* and the Trafficking in Difference', in Ania Loomba and Martin Orkin (eds.), *Postcolonial Shakespeares* (London, 1998), 43–63.

20. Everett, 'Spanish *Othello*', 740.

21. See Jonathan Dollimore, *Sexual Dissidence* (Oxford, 1991), 157–62.

22. Hugh Quarshie, *Second Thoughts About Othello* (Chipping Camden, 1999), 5–11.

23. Ben Okri, 'Leaping out of Shakespeare's Terror: Five Meditations on *Othello*', in Kwesi Owusu (ed.), *Storms of the Heart: An Anthology of Black Arts and Culture* (London, 1988), 9–18, 13.

CHAPTER 5. THE IMPERIAL ROMANCE OF *ANTONY AND CLEOPATRA*

1. 'Introduction', in Michael Neill (ed.), *Antony and Cleopatra* (Oxford, 1994), 87.

2. Peter Heylyn, *Microcosmus or A little description of the whole world* (Oxford, 1621), 387.

3. See G. K. Hunter, 'Elizabethans and Foreigners', in Catherine M. S. Alexander and Stanley Wells (eds.), *Shakespeare and Race* (Cambridge, 2000), 62–3 n. 101.

4. Lucy Hughes-Hallett, *Cleopatra, Histories, Dreams, Distortions* (London, 1990), 15, 99–100.

5. Karl H. Dannenfeldt, 'Egypt and Egyptians in the Renaissance', *Studies in the Renaissance*, 6 (1959), 7–27, 2–21.

6. Leo Africanus, *The History and Description of Africa*, ed. Robert Brown (New York, 1906), 856.

7. Henry Blount, *A Voyage into the Levant* (London 1638), 51–2. See also Geraldo U. de Sousa, *Shakespeare's Cross-Cultural Encounters* (London, 1999), 131.

8. Quoted James A. McPeek, *The Black Book of Knaves and Unthrifts* (Storres, Conn., 1969), 255.

9. Florus, quoted by Christopher Pelling, '"Anything truth can do, we can do better": the Cleopatra legend', in Susan Walker and Peter Higgs (eds.), *Cleopatra of Egypt, from History to Myth* (London, 2001), 300.

10. *The Aeneid of Virgil*, trans. Rolfe Humphries (Englewood Cliffs, NJ, 1987), 202.

11. Edward Said, *Orientalism* (London, 1978), 43, 57.

12. Andre Gunder Frank, *Re-Orient, Global Economy in the Asian Age* (Berkeley, 1998).

13. *Herodotus: the Histories* is quoted and its influence on subsequent representations of Egypt is discussed by de Sousa, *Shakespeare's Cross-Cultural Encounters*, 130–1.

14. Joannes Boemus, *The Fardle of Facions* (1555) (Amsterdam, 1970), chap. B C7^v.

15. John Bulwer, *Anthropometamorphoses, Man Transformed: or the Artificial Changeling* (London, 1653), 317–18.

16. 'Enforcing Statutes and orders for Apparel', in P. L. Hughes and J. F. Larkin (eds.), *Tudor Royal Proclamations*, iii (New Haven, 1969), 3.

17. *Hic Mulier; or the Man-Woman*, in Katherine Usher Henderson and Barbara F. Mcmanus (eds.), *Half Humankind* (Urbana, I ll., 1985), 265.

18. *The Complete Essays of Montaigne*, trans. Donald M. Frame (Stanford, Calif., 1965), 791; second emphasis added.

19. John Knox, *The first blast of the trumpet against the monstrous regiment of women* (Geneva, 1558), 13^r.

20. See Heather James, *Shakespeare's Troy: Drama, Politics and the Translation of Empire* (Cambridge, 1997), 18–20.

21. See pp. 61–2.

22. Kim Hall, 'Sexual Politics and Cultural identity in *The Masque of Blackness*', in Sue-Ellen Case and Janelle Reinelt (eds.), *The Performance of Power* (Iowa City, 1991), 14–15.

23. George Pettie, *A Petite Pallace* (London, 1590), 61.

24. Robert Greene, *Ciceronis Amor* (London, 1589), 26–7.

25. I am indebted to various critics who have commented on the connection between gypsies and Egyptians, particularly McPeek, *The Black Book*, 252–86; Charles Whitney, 'Charmian's Laughter: Women, Gypsies and

Festive Ambivalence in *Antony and Cleopatra*', *The Upstart Crow*, 14 (1994), 67–88, and de Sousa, *Shakespeare's Cross-Cultural Encounters*, ch. 5.

26. John Cowell, *The Interpreter, or Book Containing the Signification of Words* (Cambridge, 1607) Bb1^{r-v}, also quoted de Sousa, *Shakespeare's Cross-Cultural Encounters*, 143.

27. John Florio, *A Worlde of Wordes* (London, 1598); *The Complete Essays of Montaigne*, 40.

28. Thomas Dekker, *Lanthorne and Candle-Light*, in Arthur F. Kinney (ed.) *Rogues, Vagabonds and Sturdy Beggars* (Amherst, Mass., 1990), 243.

29. H. T. Crofton, 'Early Annals of the Gypsies in England', *Journal of the Gypsy Lore Society* 1: 1 (July 1889), 6.

30. Samuel Rid, *The Art of Juggling* (Amsterdam and Norwood, NJ, 1974), B2^r.

31. Kittredge, *Witchcraft in Old and New England*, quoted by McPeek, *The Black Book*, 275.

32. 5 Elizabeth C.20 (1652), in Danby Pickering (ed.), *The Statutes at Large* (Cambridge, 1763), 211.

33. The official report of the Yorkshire Quarter Sessions is quoted by McPeek, *The Black Book*, 264.

34. See also Dympna Callaghan, *Shakespeare Without Women, Repesenting Gender and Race on the Renaissance Stage* (London, 2000).

35. Edward Hall, *Chronicles*, quoted by McPeek, *The Black Book*, 257.

36. *Thomas Platter's Travels in England* (London, 1937), 192.

37. Donald F. Lach, *Asia in the Making of Europe* vol. ii, bk. 1 (Chicago, 1970), 102.

38. Crofton, 'Early Annals', 23.

CHAPTER 6. RELIGION, MONEY, AND RACE IN
THE MERCHANT OF VENICE

1. Salman Rushdie, *The Moor's Last Sigh* (London, 1995), 114–15.

2. Edmund Spenser, *A View of the Present State of Ireland*, in Henry Morley (ed.), *Ireland under Elizabeth and James the First* (London, 1890), 82.

3. See Carolyn Prager, 'The Negro Allusion in The Merchant of Venice', *American Notes and Queries*, 15: 4 (1976), 50–2; and Kim Hall, 'Guess Who's Coming to Dinner? Colonization and Miscegenation in *The Merchant of Venice*', *Renaissance Drama*, ns 23 (1992).

4. Lars Engle, *Shakespearean Pragmatism: Market of his Time* (Chicago, 1993), 101–2.

5. *Of Monsters and Prodigies* in *The Collected Works of Ambroise Paré*, facsimile of 1634 edn., (Pound Ridge, NY, 1968), 978.

6. Hakluyt, *The Principal Navigations* (Glasgow, 1903–05), vii. 262. Discussed earlier in Ch. 2.

7. Thomas Lupton, *A Thousand Notable Things of Sundrie Sorts* (London, 1579), vi. 156–7.

8. James Shapiro, *Shakespeare and the Jews* (New York, 1996), 33–4. I am indebted to Shapiro's incisive analysis throughout this chapter.

9. William Thomas, *The History of Italy*, ed. George B. Parks (Ithaca, NY, 1963), 10.

10. See David C. McPherson, *Shakespeare, Jonson, and the Myth of Venice* (Newark, Del., 1990), 61–8.

11. See Stephen Greenblatt, 'Marlowe, Marx and Anti-Semitism', in *Learning to Curse* (New York, 1990), 40–1.

12. Samuel Purchas, *Hakluytus Posthumus, or Purchas His Pilgrimes* (Glasgow, 1905), i. 325–6.

13. Jane S. Gerber, *The Jews of Spain* (New York, 1992), 150.

14. Nicholas de Nicholay, *The Navigations, Peregrinations and Voyages Made into Turkey*, trans. T. Washington the younger (London, 1585), 130.

15. Christopher Marlowe, *The Jew of Malta*, ed. James R. Siemon (London, 1994), 2. 3. 176–8, 184–99, 222–3.

16. *The Play of the Sacrament*, in *Non-Cycle Plays and Fragments*, ed. Norman Davis (London and New York, 1970), l. 196.

17. John Foxe, *Acts and Monuments* (London, 1641), 963.

18. Peter Heylyn, *Microcosmus or A little description of the whole world* (Oxford, 1621), 319.

19. John Florio, *A Worlde of Wordes* (1598) (Hildeshein, 1972), 216. See Shapiro, *Shakespeare and the Jews*, 18.

20. Thomas Calvert, *The Blessed Jew of Marocco or a Blackamoor Made White* (York, 1649), 15.

21. Quoted Gerber, *The Jews of Spain*, 165.

22. 'Part of a Letter of Master William Biddulph from Aleppo', in Purchas, *Hakluytus Posthumus*, viii. 271

23. Leo Africanus, *History and Description of Africa*, 477.

24. 'The Travels and Most Miserable Captivity of William Davies' (1614), in Thomas Osborne, *A Collection of Voyages and Travels* (London, 1745), i. 485.

25. Alan Harris Cutler and Helen Elmquist Cutler, *The Jew as an Ally of the Muslim* (Notre Dame, Ind., 1986), 2 and *passim*.

26. Sander Gilman, *Difference and Pathology: Stereotypes of Sexuality, Race and Madness* (Ithaca, NY, 1985), 31.

27. See p. 68.

28. G. K. Hunter, 'Elizabethans and Foreigners', Catherine M. S. Alexander and Stanley Wells (eds.), *Shakespeare and Race* (Cambridge, 2000), 56; McPherson, *Shakespeare, Jonson, and the Myth of Venice*, 67. See also discussion of this subject by Shapiro, *Shakespeare and the Jews*, 77–88.

29. Jerome Friedman, 'Jewish Conversion: The Spanish Pure Blood Laws and Reformation', *Sixteenth Century Journal*, 18: 1 (Spring 1987), 3–29.

30. Robert C. Stacey, 'The Conversion of Jews to Christianity in Thirteenth-Century England', *Speculum* 67 (Apr. 1992), 263–83, 278.

31. Peter Berek, 'The Jew as Renaissance Man', *Renaissance Quarterly*, 51: 1 (Spring 1998), 128–62, 132.

32. Cutler and Cutler, *The Jew as an Ally of the Muslim*, 98.

33. 'Master Brerewoods's 'Enquiries of the Religions Professed in the World', in Purchas, *Hakluytus Posthumus*, i. 324.

34. Shapiro, *Shakespeare and the Jews*, 156. Shapiro also discusses at some length definitions of Jewish identity during this period.

35. Karl Marx, *Capital* (vol. i) trans. Ben Fowkes (New York, 1977), 915.

36. See Shapiro, *Shakespeare and the Jews*, 98–100.

37. Thomas Wilson, *A Discourse Upon Usury* (1572) intro. R. H. Tawney (New York, n.d.), 205, 369.

38. Walter Cohen, 'The Merchant of Venice and the Possibilities of Historical Criticism', *ELH* 49 (1982), 765–89.

39. For a incisive reading of Marx's writings on the 'Jewish question' and their relation to Renaissance theatre, see Greenblatt, 'Marlowe, Marx and Anti-Semitism'.

40. Theodore B. Leinwand, *Theatre, Finance and Society in Early Modern England* (Cambridge, 1999), 16–17.

41. Ibid. 16.

42. For a provocative reading of the play in the context of post-Armada venturing see ibid., ch. 4.

43. Quoted John Hale, *The Civilization of Europe in the Renaissance* (New York, 1993), 150.

44. Purchas, *Hakluytus Posthumus*, i. p. xl.

45. Ibid. 244.

46. Marx, *Capital*, i. 915, 918, 926–7. See also Kenneth R. Andrews, *Trade, Plunder and Settlement* (Cambridge, 1984).

47. Marx, *Capital*, i. 229–30.

48. Mary Janell Metzger, ' "Now by My Hood, a Gentle and no Jew": Jessica, The Merchant of Venice and the Discourse of Early Modern English Identity', *PMLA* 113: 1 (Jan. 1998), 52–63.

49. Ibid. 59.

50. Peter Heylyn, *Microcosmus, or a little description of the great world* (Oxford, 1621), 236.

51. *The Discovery and Conquest of the Molucco and Philippine Islands* (London, 1708), 4.

52. See Engle, *Shakespearean Pragmatism*, 85, 92–8.

53. David Nirenberg, *Communities of Violence, Persecution of Minorities in the Middle Ages* (Princeton, 1996), 131. In the following paragraph, I am drawing upon Nirenberg's conclusions.

54. Shapiro, *Shakespeare and the Jews*, 132.

55. Browne's *Pseudodoxia Epidemeca* (1646) is cited by Shapiro, *Shakespeare and the Jews*, 276 n. 23; Bulwer, *Anthropometamorphoses* (London, 1653), 378.

56. Samuel Purchas, *Purchas His Pilgrimage or Relations of the World* (London, 1617), 165.

CONCLUSION. PLAYING WITH SHAKESPEARE

1. *The Complete Essays of Montaigne*, trans. Donald M. Frame (Stanford, Calif., 1989), 30.

2. Most notably, Francis Barker and Peter Hulme, 'Nymphs and Reapers Heavily Vanish: The Discursive Con-Texts of *The Tempest*', in John Drakakis (ed.), *Alternative Shakespeares* (London, 1985), 206–27; Paul Brown, '"This Thing of Darkness I Acknowledge Mine": *The Tempest* and the Discourse of Colonialism', in Jonathan Dollimore and Alan Sinfield (eds.), *Political Shakespeare* (Manchester, 1985), 48–71.

3. Octavio Mannoni, *Prospero and Caliban: The Psychology of Colonization* trans. P. Powesland (London, 1956); first published in French in 1950.

4. Roberto Fernández Retamar, 'Caliban: Notes Towards a Discussion of Culture in Our America', *Massachusetts Review* 15 (1974), 7–72.

5. Aimé Césaire, *Une Tempête* (Paris, 1969).

6. Frantz Fanon, *Black Skin, White Masks*, trans. Charles Lam Markmann (New York, 1967); first published 1952.

7. George Lamming, *The Pleasures of Exile* (London, 1984); first published 1960.

8. See Ania Loomba, *Gender, Race, Renaissance Drama* (Manchester, 1989), 142–58; and Peter Hulme and William H. Sherman (eds.), *'The Tempest' and its Travels* (London, 2000).

9. Peter Hulme, 'Reading from Elsewhere: George Lamming and the Paradox of Exile', in Hulme and Sherman (eds.), *'The Tempest' and its Travels*, 220–35.

10. Stephen Greenblatt, 'Learning to Curse: Aspects of Linguistic Colonialism in the Sixteenth Century', in *Learning to Curse* (New York, 1990), 31.

11. The play has been appropriated all over the world but it is the Caribbean rewritings have been the most powerful, numerous, and, lately, the most visible in postcolonial as well as early modern criticism.

12. See Ania Loomba, 'Shakespeare and Cultural Difference', in Terence Hawkes (ed.), *Alternative Shakespeares*, ii (London, 1994), 164–91.

13. *The Tempest*, ed. Stephen Orgel (Oxford, 1987), 41.

14. Jerry Brotton, '"This Tunis, sir, was Carthage": Contesting Colonialism in *The Tempest*', in Ania Loomba and Martin Orkin (eds.), *Postcolonial Shakespeares* (London, 1998), 23–42, 34.

15. Leo Africanus, *The History and Description of Africa*, ed. Robert Brown (New York, 1906), 716.

16. See also Barbara Fuchs, 'Conquering Islands: Contextualizing *The Tempest*', *Shakespeare Quarterly* 48: 1 (Spring 1997), 45–62.

17. The Irish dimensions were hinted at by Paul Brown, '"This Thing of Darkness"'; and uncovered by numerous critics such as Ronald Takaki, '*The Tempest* in the Wilderness: The Racialization of Savagery', *Journal of American History* 79: 3 (Dec. 1992); and David J. Baker, 'Where is Ireland in *The Tempest*?', in Mark Thronton Burnett and Ramona Wray (eds.), *Shakespeare and Ireland* (London, 1997), 68–88; and most suggestively by Dympna Callaghan, *Shakespeare Without Women* (London, 2000).

18. Peter Berek, 'The Jew as Renaissance Man', *Renaissance Quarterly* 51: 1 (Spring 1998), 128–62, makes the point in relation to Jews; Nabil Matar, *Turks, Moors and Englishmen in the Age of Discovery* (New York, 1999), 13, suggests the same in the case of Moors.

The following books and essays are useful for thinking about race as a concept: Robert Miles, *Racism* (London, 1989); Étienne Balibar and Immanuel Wallerstein, *Race, Nation, Class: Ambiguous Identities* (London, 1991); Stephen Jay Gould, *The Mismeasure of Man* (New York, 1996); *Sociological Theories, Race and Colonialism* (Paris, 1980); Sander Gilman, *Difference and Pathology, Stereotypes of Sexuality, Race and Madness* (Ithaca, NY, and London, 1985); David Theo Goldberg (ed.), *The Anatomy of Racism* (Minneapolis and London, 1990); Frantz Fanon, *Black Skin, White Masks* (New York, 1967). Edward W. Said, *Orientalism* (London, 1978) details the intellectual consequences of colonial thought. On the idea of nation, generally, as well as in early modern England, see Benedict Anderson, *Imagined Communities, Reflections on the Origin and Spread of Nationalism* (London, 1991); Nira Yuval-Davis and Floya Anthias (eds.), *Woman-Nation-State* (London, 1989); Liah Greenfeld, *Nationalism: Five Roads to Modernity* (Cambridge, Mass., 1992); Richard Helgerson, *Forms of Nationhood: The Elizabethan Writing of England* (Chicago and London, 1992); and Jean Howard and Phyllis Rackin, *Engendering a Nation* (New York, 1997).

On race in the medieval and early modern periods, excellent starting points are *Journal of Medieval and Early Modern Studies* 31: 1 (2001); and *William and Mary Quarterly*, 3rd ser., 54: 1 (Jan. 1997). Martin Bernal's *Black Athena: The Afroasiatic Roots of Classical Civilization* (New Brunswick, NJ, 1987) offers a revisionist account of classical Greece. For medieval contexts see also Robert Bartlett, *The Making of Europe, Conquest, Colonization and Cultural Change 950–1350* (Princeton, 1993); *The Postcolonial Middle Ages* (New York, 2000); Dorothee Metlitzki, *The Matter of Araby in Medieval England* (New Haven and London, 1977); and David Nirenberg, *Communities of Violence, Persecution of Minorities in the Middle Ages* (Princeton, 1996). On blackness and difference in the early modern period, see Peter Fryer, *Staying Power: The History of Black People in Britain* (London, 1984); Eldred Jones, *Othello's Countrymen* (London, 1965); Anthony Barthelemy, *Black Face, Maligned Race* (Baton Rouge, La., 1987); Elliot H. Tokson, *The Popular Image of the Black Man in English Drama 1550–1688* (Boston, 1982); Jack D'Amico, *The Moor in English*

Renaissance Drama (Tampa, Fla., 1991); John Gillies, *Shakespeare and the Geography of Difference* (Cambridge, 1994).

Kim F. Hall, *Things of Darkness: Economies of Race and Gender in Early Modern England* (Ithaca, NY, 1995) is the most comprehensive in interrelating the development of racial and gender ideologies; see also Ania Loomba, *Gender, Race, Renaissance Drama* (Manchester, 1989); Karen Newman, *Fashioning Femininity and English Renaissance Drama* (Chicago, 1991); Patricia Parker and Margo Hendricks (eds.), *Women, 'Race' and Writing in the Early Modern Period* (London, 1994); Geraldo U. de Sousa, *Shakespeare's Cross-Cultural Encounters* (London, 1999); and Dympna Callaghan, *Shakespeare Without Women; Representing Gender and Race on the Renaissance Stage* (London, 2000).

Catherine M. S. Alexander and Stanley Wells (eds.), *Shakespeare and Race* (Cambridge, 2000) shows how the subject has developed over time. Other useful collections are Joyce Green MacDonald (ed.), *Race, Ethnicity, and Power in the Renaissance* (Madison, 1997); Jean-Pierre Maquerlot and Michèle Willems, *Travel and Drama in Shakespeare's Time* (Cambridge, 1996); and Peter Erickson and Clark Hulse (eds.), *Early Modern Visual Culture: Representation, Race and Empire in Renaissance England* (Philadelphia, 2000).

The following books on New World contexts set the agenda for studies of early modern colonialism: Peter Hulme, *Colonial Encounters, Europe and the Native Caribbean 1492–1797* (London, 1986); Stephen Greenblatt, *Learning to Curse* (New York, 1990) and *Marvellous Possessions: The Wonder of the New World* (Chicago, 1991); Stephen Greenblatt (ed.), *New World Encounters* (Berkeley, 1993). On Ireland and colonization see Brendan Bradshaw, Andrew Hadfield, and Willy Maley (eds.), *Representing Ireland, Literature and Origins of Conflict, 1534–1660* (Cambridge, 1993) and Mark Thronton Burnett and Ramona Wray (eds.), *Shakespeare and Ireland* (London, 1997). On Islam and the East, Samuel Chew, *The Crescent and the Rose, Islam and England During the Renaissance* (New York, 1937) remains indispensable. Newer work is represented by Nabil Matar, *Turks, Moors and Englishmen in the Age of Discovery* (New York, 1999), and *Islam in Britain* (Cambridge, 1998); Daniel J. Vitkus, 'Turning Turk in *Othello*: The Conversion and Damnation of the Moor', *Shakespeare Quarterly* 48: 2 (Summer 1997), 145–76. On Jews, by far the most comprehensive is James Shapiro, *Shakespeare and the Jews* (New York, 1996). Mary Janell Metzger, ' "Now by My Hood, a Gentle and no Jew": Jessica, *The Merchant of Venice* and the Discourse of Early Modern English Identity', *PMLA* 113: 1 (Jan. 1998), 52–63, provides an important focus on issues of gender.

Books on early modern trade and colonialism are too numerous to list here, but the multiple volumes of Donald Lach's *Asia in the Making of Europe* (Chicago, 1968–94) extensively map contact between Asia and Europe, and include comprehensive bibliographies. John Archer, *Old Worlds: Egypt, Southwest Asia, India and Russia in Early Modern English Writing* and Shankar Raman, *Framing 'India': The Colonial Imaginary in Early Modern Culture* (both Stanford, 2001) are important in reorienting literary scholarship towards the East. Virginia Mason Vaughan's *Shakespeare's Caliban: A Cultural History* (Cambridge, 1991) and *Othello: A Contextual History* (Cambridge, 1994) are exemplary in bringing multiple geographical and historical contexts to bear upon single Shakespearian texts. Race and postcoloniality are explored by Martin Orkin, *Shakespeare against Apartheid* (Craighall, 1987); Ania Loomba and Martin Orkin (eds.), *Postcolonial Shakespeares* (London, 1998); Thomas Cartelli, *Repositioning Shakespeare* (London, 1999); and David Johnson, *Shakespeare and South Africa* (Oxford, 1997).

Index

Printed and bound by CPI Group (UK) Ltd, Croydon, CR0 4YY